# BIRD IN THE BUSH

# OTHER BOOKS BY KENNETH REXROTH

# BIRD IN THE BUSH

*OBVIOUS ESSAYS BY*

# KENNETH REXROTH

*A NEW DIRECTIONS PAPERBOOK*

The author and the publisher acknowledge with thanks permission to re-print the following material, which first appeared in the magazines or books named. Some of the titles have been changed.

"Unacknowledged Legislators and *Art pour Art*", was first delivered as a speech at the Library School of the University of Southern California, and then appeared in *Artesian* magazine, Fall 1958, published by Great Lakes Publishers.

"Some Thoughts on Jazz as Music, as Revolt, as Mystique", *New World Writing #14*, published by The New American Library of World Literature, Inc.

"The Reality of Henry Miller", first published as an Introduction to *Nights of Love and Laughter* by Henry Miller, published in a Signet edition by The New American Library of World Literature, Inc.

"The Visionary Painting of Morris Graves", *Perspectives USA #10*, pub-lished by Intercultural Publications Inc.

"Turner: Painting as an Organism of Light", *The Art Digest*, February 1955.

"Mark Tobey: Painter of the Humane Abstract", *Art News*, May 1951.

"The Heroic Object and Fernand Léger", *Art News*, October 1953.

"The Plays of Yeats" was originally heard over station KPFA, San Fran-cisco.

All of the following essays first appeared in *The Nation*, in the issues noted: "The Chinese Classic Novel in Translation", April 14, 1956; "Would You Hit a Woman with a Child", April 27, 1957; "The Ennobling Revul-sion", July 20, 1957; "Rimbaud as Capitalist Adventurer", October 12, 1957; "The International Industrial Development Conference", November 2, 1957; "Samuel Beckett and the Importance of Waiting", December 7, 1957; and "My Head Gets Tooken Apart", December 14, 1957.

Design by Stefan Salter

Manufactured in the United States of America

New Directions books are published by James Laughlin
New York Office—333 Sixth Avenue (14)

# CONTENTS

# INTRODUCTION

Practicing writers and artists notoriously have very little use for critics. I am a practicing writer and artist. Long ago Edmund Wilson is reputed to have said that a critic was a book reviewer who wrote for magazines that paid little or nothing.

These pieces are not criticism but journalism. It is my hope that they find a modest place in what critics call a "tradition"—the tradition of Huneker, Mencken, Wilson. Not one of them has ever appeared in a Quarterly. They were all assigned in advance, written to a requested wordage and for an agreed fee. Otherwise I would never have written them. Poets are very ill advised to write prose for anything but money. The only possible exceptions are anger and logrolling for one's friends.

Curiously enough, this is the only approach that permits the writer any freedom. As long as you avoid outright libel or misrepresentation of known fact, the better-class newspapers and slick magazines let you write pretty much what you want. They are interested in lively, engaging copy, and within reason, the more controversy the better. The Quarterlies and Critical Reviews, on the other hand, have a Party Line of unbelievable rigidity. It is a subtle blend of bankrupt, sectarian Bolshevism, the Ku Klux Klan, the provincialism of the subway Neanderthals, and the more blatant propaganda of the State Department. Furthermore, they permit not the slightest deviation from the canons of taste evolved at last year's cocktail parties.

Taste is an individual thing. If it is not wide-ranging and erratic, captious and unpredictable, it is not taste but snobbery. Just try saying: Mark Twain is a better writer than Henry James. The 10th Street Club is the apotheosis of formularized academic painting. Kierkegaard is dull and silly. No adult can take Dostoevsky seriously. Pissaro was a better painter than Van Gogh and Tiepolo than El Greco, who is another artist for adolescents. *Finnegans Wake* is an embarrassing failure. You can't associate continuously with immature minds and write poetry—even if it's called Creative Poetry 1976520 A and you get paid $18,000 a year for it. . . . Just say anything like that and see how far you get with Phil Rahv.

These essays are all jobs, except the one on Buber which I wrote to organize my own relationship to a thinker who has had a major influence on me. I might not have chosen these subjects if I had just been criticizing for fun. I prefer Tiepolo, Redon, Pissaro—or Ernest Briggs—to Léger. I think Lawrence a very great poet indeed, but a rather disgusting man, afraid of wildcats, red Indians, and children, who deliberately wrote erotic novels and then got up and left the room in a blushing rage when somebody told a dirty joke. There is a lot of bullshit in Lawrence, Miller, or Patchen—but their enemies are my enemies.

Everybody has a lot of fakery in his make-up. When it is personal it is all right. A man can be forgiven for being a snarf, a vegetarian, or a frequenter of astrologists. He cannot be forgiven for being a parson or a social worker or a professor. No truck with the Social Lie. Why not? Not because it makes you a partner in mass murder, which it does, but because it reduces all action to frivolity.

Once moral authority is delegated all action becomes meaningless. The institutionalization of creativity which is almost all-prevailing today is met with reluctance, secret recalcitrance, *tedium vitae*, however gaudy the rewards, or even however noble the ends. Reluctant engineers can build Dnieprestroy, reluctant intellectuals can implement Mr. Dulles' lethal priggery in Taiwan, Spain, or Santo Domingo. You cannot write a reluctant poem or paint a reluctant picture. Those who pretend to are, on the face of it, institutionalized imbeciles.

Most of the writing, painting, composing done in the world today, on both sides of the Cold War, is done by people whose careers are records of bone-chilling frivolity. Once it was Cubism, then Futurism, then Surrealism. The dominant school today is the Pre-Frontal Lobotomy Movement. This produces framed canvases carefully painted all over to represent empty space, columns of type indented on both margins and written by Professors of Creative

Poetry, which are really elaborately camouflaged holes in the paper. It also produces hydrogen bombs. Against the armies of the mindless I will take what few allies I can find, whatever their faults.

However, I will not take those would-be allies which Madison Avenue has carefully manufactured and is now trying to foist on me. If the only significant revolt against what the French call the *hallucination publicitaire* is heroin and Zen Buddhism nobody will ever be able to escape from the lot of this tenth-rate Russian movie called "The Collapse of Capitalist Civilization" onto which somehow we all seem to have wandered.

The Beat Generation may once have been human beings —today they are simply comical bogies conjured up by the Luce publications. Their leading spokesmen are just "Engine Charley" Wilson and Dr. Oppenheimer dressed up in scraggly beards and dirty socks. For this reason I have omitted from this collection all those articles which discussed the revolt or emotional suicide of young American writers, published back in the days when Madison Avenue and its outposts in the Quarterlies were all insisting that everything was conformity, peace, and professorships.

Success, alas, as it almost always does, led to the worst kind of emotional suicide. Those to whom that kind of success was a temptation have become the trained monkeys, the clowning helots of the Enemy. They came to us late, from the slums of Greenwich Village, and they departed early, for the salons of millionairesses.

Life with us goes on just the same. Born and raised in what they used to call "The Radical Movement" I always look back with amused pride on those old timers who didn't smoke or drink and lived long and troubled lives absolutely devoted to one unmarried spouse—to keep themselves fit and ready for the barricades. The World, The Flesh, and The Devil are far subtler personages than those innocent Jewish mechanics and Italian peasants thought, but they still go about in the night as a roaring lion seeking whom they may devour. It behoves the artist to recognize and avoid them, especially when they wave red, or black, flags, as well as roar. Because art *is* a weapon. After millions of well-aimed blows, someday perhaps it will break the stone heart of the mindless cacodemon called Things As They Are. Everything else has failed.

KENNETH REXROTH

# BIRD IN THE BUSH

# UNACKNOWLEDGED
# LEGISLATORS AND
# *ART POUR ART*

The oldest and most popular subject of criticism is apparently the role of poetry and the place of the poet in society. The arguments of Plato and Aristotle are not early but late. Long before their day, on Egyptian papyrus and Babylonian clay tablet and in the Prophetic Books of the Bible, the discussion was going on. As most of you may know, Plato had a very low opinion of poets. Isaiah had a very exalted one. From those days to the present the debate has continued.

In most cases the dispute has been so disputatious because so many of the participants have had a very inadequate idea of the nature of poetry, what it actually is, how it achieves its effects, what the arts do generally in and with society. I think the best way to start is naïvely and empirically to say that poetry is what poets write and poets are what the public generally agrees are poets. In my time anthologists have included everybody from Walter Pater to Vanzetti to Thomas Wolfe amongst the poets, but actually very few people would accept this judgment. Florid prose is not poetry; in fact it is often very close to being the opposite of poetry, rhetoric. The public seems to sense this. The Dadaist poetry of Tristan Tzara is considered poetry, even by people who neither like nor understand it. The last page of the *Garden of Cyrus* of Sir Thomas Browne or the sermons of Donne are beautiful rhetoric.

Let us start with a poet whose social responsibility is not very manifest. He wrote during the few brief years that the Roman Republic broke down once and for all and Julius Caesar began the organization of the Empire which came into full existence under Augustus, a period of economic booms and crises, of civil war and the constant threat of social revolution both from the upper and the lower classes. What have the poems of Catullus to do with either Republic or Empire, with the social collapse and conflict he saw about him? Is there any evidence that he interfered in any way with the society of his time? He wrote a lot of obscene and abusive poems about Julius Caesar, Mamurra, Mentulus, the millionaires of the "popular" cause. They were personally motivated—he just didn't like them. Actually, he seems to have belonged to their circle. He certainly did not belong to the Senatorial party.

You could say that his poetry reflects passively the first period of Roman decadence, the breakdown of the caste system, the fall of the Republic, the spread of the Empire far beyond the Italian peninsula, the looting of the East, the emergence of the little circle of families of tremendous wealth, the dying out of the old stern ideal of Republican morality, the spread of a public and a private morality much like that of our own Hollywood or Café Society, through all classes. It is always presumed that the Lesbia of his most passionate love poems was Clodia, one of the more notorious evil livers of all time, a multi-millionaire courtesan like those who are always in our own newspapers. You could write a whole book like this and run it serially in *Pravda*, and you wouldn't have said anything important.

Nobody has ever valued Catullus for such things, from Clodia or Caesar to our own day. Men have read him all these years and will continue to read him for his peculiarly exacerbated sensibility, the fine sharpness of his perception, the clarity and splendor of his language, and the heartbreaking pathos of—not the emotions he describes—but the actual emotional situations he recreates for us with such power, the drama of his own life in which he is able to involve us directly, as though it were our own.

This is certainly one of the things poetry does. It communicates the most intense experiences of very highly developed sensibilities. With whom does it communicate? Like any published utterance it communicates out into society with anyone who wants to be communicated with. The poet may envisage a specific audience, exquisites like himself, the proletariat, the "folk"—but actually he broadcasts and takes his chances with an audience.

Perhaps this is enough. As time goes on and the poem is absorbed by more and more people, it performs historically and socially the function of a symbolic criticism of values. It widens and deepens and sharpens the sensibility and overcomes that dullness to significant experience that the Jesuits used to call "invincible ignorance." People are by and large routinized in their lives. A great many of

5

our responses to experience are necessarily dulled. If to a certain extent they weren't, we'd all suffer from nervous breakdowns and die of high blood pressure at the age of twenty. The organism has to protect itself. It cannot be completely raw.

What the arts do, and particularly what the most highly organized art of speech does, is to develop and refine this very rawness and make it selective. Poetry increases and guides our awareness to immediate experience and to the generalizations which can be made from immediate experience. It organizes sensibility so that it is not wasted. Unorganized sensibility is simply irritability. If every sense impression, every emotion, every response were as acute as it could be, we would soon go to pieces. The arts build in us scales and hierarchies of response.

As acuteness grows and becomes more organized in the individual and in society as a whole—in the separate individuals who make up the abstraction "society as a whole" —it reorganizes and restates the general value judgments of the society. We become more clearly aware of what is good and bad, interesting and dull, beautiful and ugly, lovable and mean. Experience thus comes to have greater scope, greater depth, greater intensity. Many activities of man do this—but it is specifically, primarily, the function of poetry.

Whatever else the arts do, and amongst them the art of poetry, this is the simplest and most obvious thing. If we stick to this we push aside a great deal of aesthetic argument. Is art—or poetry—communication or construction?

Criticism in the recent past has held that the arts are largely construction, and that it is the architectonics of the construction which provide the criteria of judgment. All the arts were assimilated to the canons of architecture and music. Of course, the answer to this is that Chartres or the Parthenon are not purely construction. All great architecture, like all music, is very definitely a kind of communication. The Parthenon says something, something quite different from what Santa Sophia says centuries later. This should be self-evident—San Vitale, Saint Front, Albi, Lincoln Cathedral, Richardson's Trinity Church, the UN Building—these are overpowering acts of communication, each widely different from the rest.

Purposive construction of any kind is a species of communication, just as any kind of communication must be structured. I cannot get paid for this lecture * by babbling to you incoherently.

From the opposite aesthetic direction there has come in recent years, in the art of painting especially and to a lesser degree in poetry and music, the exploitation of what is called "the art of random occasion." People spill paint on canvas, ink their shoes and walk on paper, stare at a glittering point and write down their "free associations." Now the actual purpose of such activity is to show the kind of communication that emerges, under the guidance of the sensibility and taste of the artist, even out of the manipulation of accident. After all, nothing looks so much like a

---

* This essay was first presented as a lecture at the University of Southern California Library in May, 1958.

Jackson Pollock as another Jackson Pollock. This can be said of the work of all the abstract expressionists. As painting has exploited more and more the manipulation of random occasion, the more personal the paintings have become. I am not arguing about the ultimate value of Rothko, or Still, or Motherwell. I do not as a matter of fact think this is the very highest kind of painting. I am simply pointing out that any familiarity with it reveals how strongly personal, how individually communicative it is.

Is it that when you have a minimum of active construction and a maximum of chance and "inspiration" the unconscious mind operates to reveal the artist more intimately? I think not. The poetry of Paul Valéry and T. S. Eliot is presented as rigorously constructed, unemotional, impersonal—"like the Parthenon." Like the Parthenon it turns out to be intensely personal. At the first glance at the page, Pope seems to be the most formal of poets. The sentences unroll in strict balance and antithesis, the couplets always carefully scanned. He is the perfect example of absolute obedience to eighteenth-century French aesthetic theories. But what happens when you pay attention to the poetry? There emerges a tortured neurotic, shivering with a kind of exquisite irritability, one of the most personal utterances in literature. T. S. Eliot has told us all so many times that he has no emotion, that he never writes of personal experience. The truth is that his poetry is so personal that you can reconstruct his whole inner life, his whole personal history, from it. It is as embarrassingly intimate as the revelations of the analyst's couch. Remember when he climbs the winding stair and looks out through the keyhole window and sees Spring on Westminster Place in St. Louis, and the flowering bushes, and all the agony of childhood? Valéry too says there is no emotion, no "expression, no personality, no direct communication" in his work. It is just architecture and music. And then, in *The Marine Cemetery*, he cries out, "Ah, Zenon! Cruel Zenon d'Elée!" and the pathos of this man caught in the trap of his own gospel of implacable order overwhelms you, the torture of this mind hiding behind its formalism is almost more than you can bear.

In poetry, as in all the arts, both the constructive and communicative aspects are tremendously raised in power, but they do not differ in kind from ordinary speech. Only the aesthetician who brings to the arts considerations from elsewhere in philosophy, from ontology or epistemology, can postulate a different realm of being with its own kind of communication in poetry. Hector with his wife and child, Piccarda's speech to Dante, the ghost of Hamlet's father, these are all, however exalted, in the same world as "Please pass the butter." Furthermore, medìeval and "vulgar" aesthetics are perfectly right when they speak, as Plato and Aristotle did, of the Art of Cooking, or the Art of the Saddler. The only difference in the Fine Arts is that they are finer—and they communicate more, and more importantly. Albi Cathedral is the sum total of the work of its bricklayers as well as of the plans of its architects. As construction, the difference is simply one of degree. There is no sure point at which you can say, "Beyond is Fine Art."

9

Instead in the constructive activities of men you have a continuum, growing in refinement, intensity, scope, depth, and splendor. Here Thomas Aquinas and his modern followers are right.

Furthermore, certain works of art in recent years have taught us that you can apprehend even the simplest speech or simplest plastic arrangement, or, to take somebody like Webern, even a fugue on two notes, with the intensity of an artistic experience if you want to compel yourself to do it. Yoga and other mystical gymnastics involving the faculties of attention have always done this. You all know the modern photographs of hop-scotch squares on sidewalks, torn signboards, broken windows, piles of lumber, and similar things. What the photographer is doing is focusing attention on something that was not actually structured in the first place. It is the attention which creates the structure. You can train yourself to see the clouds of Tiepolo, the mists and mountains of Sesshu, in any water-stained ceiling.

Gertrude Stein did this with words. You say poetry is different, disinterested and structured. It is not the same kind of thing as "Please pass the butter," which is a simple imperative. But Gertrude Stein showed, among other things, that if you focus your attention on "Please pass the butter," and put it through enough permutations and combinations, it begins to take on a kind of glow, the splendor of what is called an "aesthetic object," and passes over into abstract, architectonic poetry. This is a trick of the manipulation of attention. Pages and pages of Gertrude Stein are put together out of the most trivial speech, broken up and used "architecturally" to the point that ordinary meaning disappears, not from the sentences, but from the very words themselves, and a new, rather low-grade but also rather uncanny kind of meaning emerges. I happen to think that her work was valuable. It makes interesting reading for a while, but it is, by and large, a failure, because it lacks enough significant contrast to engage the attention for long. Besides, her interests, her conclusions about life, her ideas about almost anything, are so terribly pedestrian.

To get back: what kind of communication are we dealing with in the arts? So much of our dispute about what poetry does, about what happens between poet and hearer or reader is due to old unsolved questions about the nature of knowledge and the nature of communication. This whole body of argument is peculiar to the Western world during the last three hundred years. The philosopher I. A. Richards once wrote a book, *Mencius on the Mind*, all about how the classical Chinese philosophers spent a great deal of time discussing epistemology, the problems of knowledge and communication. It is a very ingenious book, but it is untrue. What we call the epistemological dilemmas of modern thought have never existed for anybody except Western man. The whole problem of knowledge and communication never bothered other people in other civilizations. We forget that to a very large degree it does not bother the bulk of the people of Western civilization either. The epistemological problem arose as in Europe and America human relationships became increasingly abstract, and the relation of men to their work became more remote. Six

11

men who have worked together to build a boat or a house with their own hands do not doubt its existence.

As human beings grow more remote from one another, they become more like things than persons to each other. As this happens the individual becomes remote from, *loses,* himself. First alienation from comradeship in the struggle with nature, then alienation from each other, finally self-alienation. A great deal of our communication is not with persons at all. It might just as well be a machine to which we say "Pass the butter." What we want is the butter. This is what people mean when they say the communication of the arts is of a different kind. But this is not communication at all, it is verbal manipulation of the world of things. "Reification" an American philosopher once called it. The arts presume to speak directly from person to person, each polarity, the person at each end of the communication fully realized. The speech of poetry is from me to you, transfigured by the overcoming of all thingness—reification—in the relationship. So speech approaches in poetry not only the directness and the impact but the unlimited potential of act. A love poem is an act of communication of love, like a kiss. The poem of contempt and satire is like a punch in the nose. The work of art has about it an immediacy of experience of the sort that many people never manage in their daily lives. At the same time it has an illimitable character. Speech between you and me is focused, but spreads off indefinitely and immeasurably. What is communicated is self to self—whole "universes of discourse." When we deal with others as instruments, as machines of our desires, we

as well as they are essentially passive and limited to the
end in view. My relationship to a horse is more active than
my relationship to a car. Something happens but it is outside of us. In the arts—and ideally in much other communication—the relationship is not only active, it is the
highest form of activity. Nothing happens. Not outside in
the world. Everything is as it was before. We react to
things, we respond to persons. In the arts we respond to the
living communication of a person, no matter how long gone
the artist may be. In a sense, out into unlimited time and
space, say from the studio of an Egyptian sculptor, the
artist is speaking, alive, to us, person to living person. Of
course it is this which is the subject of the great poems by
Horace, Shakespeare, and Gautier: "No *thing* will outlive
the living word."

No thing happens. What changes is the sensibility. It
deepens, widens, becomes more intense and complex, in the
interchange between person and person. If, historically,
this is a cumulative change, it is a very slight one. There is
no evidence that Picasso has "progressed" beyond the
paintings of the cave men of Altamira, or that Sappho is
less a poet than Christina Rossetti. Progress takes place in
the world considered as an instrument. And even here it is
questionable if tools, means of production, which irrevocably separate man from man, represent progress or decadence. I think the arts do progress, but they progress in
their means, in their own instruments and in a slow growth
towards more widespread purity, that is, lack of adultera-
tion with just this reification. Of course, from the very

13

beginning—Sappho, the songs of the *Shih Ching*—this purity exists. And the tone changes. Each age has its specific sonority, its response to its time. (The politician cannot understand this. For him all persons are things. So the lyric folk songs of the Chinese *Book of Odes,* the *Shih Ching,* were "interpreted" by the followers of Confucius as versified political homilies.)

Often the poet, let alone his audience, is not very clear about what he is doing. Consider how certain key poets in the European tradition have lifted up and crystallized and illuminated the whole thought of their epoch. This is particularly true of Baudelaire. Sometime ago I said in an article in *The Nation,* "Baudelaire was the greatest poet of the capitalist epoch. Does anybody dispute this?" Well, nobody wrote any letters. Yet Baudelaire had all sorts of idiotic ideas about why and how he wrote. But more than any other poet for two hundred years he communicated. He defined and gave expression to all the dilemmas of modern man, caught in the cruel dynamic of an acquisitive and continually disintegrating society, a society which had suddenly abandoned satisfactions which went back to the beginning of human communities in the Neolithic Age. Baudelaire, at first sight, painted the entire portrait of modern man, urban and self-alienated. He speaks directly to each of us like a twin brother. And yet Baudelaire was hardly aware of the magnitude of his accomplishment— he had such foolish ideas when he tried to explain himself.

Blake, in so many superficial ways, inanimate reification ways, the very antithesis of Baudelaire, plays a similar role

14

in the founding of the modern sensibility in English. He saw the whole picture of the oncoming nineteenth-century civilization with its dark Satanic mills. He wanted none of it, but he came to grips with it. It is very pertinent that for most tastes Blake's most powerful wrestling with his time and the future occurs in his lyrics, not in his *Prophetic Books* where he presumes to deal with such matters explicitly, or at least allegorically. This is true of Burns, a specifically Jacobin poet—a professional revolutionary in a sense. He takes a simple Scotch folk song and ever so slightly alters its hackneyed lines with the slightest shading and change of emphasis. A whole new realm of values opens up. And he is more successful in his lyrics, in my opinion, than in his long satires, admirable as those are.

The outstanding example of this social-historical role of the poet is Dryden. From the Puritan republic of Cromwell to the Roman Catholic despotism of James II, Dryden changed with the politics of his day. Each time he wrote a long poem to justify himself. It would be easy to dismiss this as timeserving, but careful reading of the poems themselves carries the conviction of Dryden's sincerity. Although he became progressively more reactionary, the whole structure of his thought, as he hammered it out in a new kind of verse and a new attitude towards reality, presages the oncoming secular, republican, rationalist eighteenth century. Out of Dryden you can deduce Gibbon or Voltaire, but you cannot even imagine Cardinal Newman. Dryden himself, of course, was completely unaware of this.

So programmatic poets do not, by and large, even speak for the programs they think they promulgate. The propaganda poet thinks of men as things and of poetry as an instrument for their manipulation. Again, consciously tendentious poets are crippled by their "message" and tend to be just that much less effective. Milton presumed to speak for the new era of Protestant middle-class republicanism. Yet his poetry is technically reactionary and looks backward to the Renaissance and even the late Middle Ages. The person we meet in Milton would have been happier in the court of that Henry VIII he despised, or of Lorenzo de' Medici a century or more before him. Who speaks for France of the first half of the nineteenth century: Lamartine? Beranger? Or Baudelaire? We do not read Shelley for his dreary rehash of the woodenly inhuman and humorless ideas of Godwin but for the developing sensibility of the oncoming century which he shares with Keats. This is his unacknowledged legislation.

It so happens that until modern times few poets were "pure poets" in George Moore's sense—completely disinterested in anything but personal communication. Most poetry in the Western world is more or less corrupted with rhetoric and manipulation . . . with program and exposition, and the actual poetry, the living speech of person to person, has been a by-product. The felicities of Dante are such by-products, of an embittered politician rewarding his friends and punishing his enemies and preaching an already outworn philosophy and cosmology and an ugly, vindictive, and cruel religion. I think Dante was much more interested in putting the "other side" in various disagreeable pits of Hell than he was in the magnificent images of the gate and the first level of Hell or in the glory of Piccarda's speech. For this reason, although passages of Dante are amongst the very greatest in all literature, he is not so great a poet as Homer or Sappho or Tu Fu. The greatest poetry cannot redeem an obnoxious creed and an unpleasant disposition.

How few poets have this purity! Horace, Catullus, Sappho, Meleager, Asclepiades, Chaucer, medieval lyricists, Shakespeare in his songs, Burns, Marvell, Landor, Blake, Li Po, Tu Fu, *The Song of Songs*—the list could be prolonged, but not very far. A poet like Tu Fu has a purity, a directness and a simplicity—presents himself immediately as a person in total communication—in a way so few Western poets do. And yet, even here this purity is partly a matter of perspective. Tu Fu never forgot his role as a court official, a censor. Even after he was fired and the T'ang court was demoralized and exiled, he went right on "admonishing the Emperor." Much of this, couched in symbols of natural occurrence, simply goes by the average reader.

However, there are rare instances where the "message," the expository occasion that floats as it were the poetic accomplishment, is itself so profound, so deep an utterance of a fully realized person that it augments the poetry and raises it to the highest level. This is certainly true of Homer as it is just as certainly not true of Dante or Milton. As you read the *Iliad* and *Odyssey*, the sublimity of the conception rises slowly through the sublimity of the language. An old man, blind now, who has known all the courts and ships and men and women of the Eastern Mediterranean, tells you, with all the conviction of total personal involvement in his speech—"The universe and its parts, the great forces of Nature, fire, sun, sky and storm, earth and procreation, viewed as persons are frivolous and dangerous, from the point of view of men often malicious, and always unpredictable. The thing that endures, that gives value to life, is comradeship, loyalty, bravery, magnanimity, love, the relations of men in direct communication with each other, personally, as persons, committed to each other. From this comes the beauty of life, its tragedy and its meaning, and from nowhere else."

The great Chinese poets say the same thing, except that they make no moral judgment of the universe. They have no gods to fight against. Man and his virtues are a part of the universe, like falling water and standing stone and drifting mist.

# SOME THOUGHTS
# ON JAZZ AS MUSIC,
# AS REVOLT,
# AS MYSTIQUE

One night, while I was doing poetry and jazz concerts at the Five Spot Café in New York, an unusually large number of old friends from my "other life" as a literary man, happened to turn up—editors, poets, novelists, journalists. They were polite and attentive, even appreciative—but they fell into two sharply distinguished classes: those who understood what was going on, musically, and those who did not understand at all—to whom it was all a closed door on a closed book in an unknown language. The latter could appreciate the poetry, they were musically literate, and could, to greater or less degree, get something out of Webern or Orlando de Lassus, and presumably they were not put off by the combination of recitative and music. They had all probably heard and liked *Façade, Persephone, Joan of Arc,* and other modern combinations of the spoken word and orchestral music. What was shutting them off was specifically jazz. They were a small minority, but the absoluteness of their reaction gave them a disproportionate importance, that and the fact that their positions in the intellectual life of the city would lead normally to the assumption that they would be accessible. The two most

19

uncomprehending were both on the staffs of important magazines, highbrow men-about-town who must have been exposed to jazz off and on for thirty years, and most of whose friends are jazz buffs of varying degrees of sophistication. One thought a long flowing samba was "boogie-woogie." The other objector thought it was all just a lot of discords with no rhythm at all.

This led to one of those discussions of fundamentals that get nowhere—least of all in night clubs. Arabel Porter, who seemed to be enjoying it, suggested that I write a sort of primer of jazz for the next issue of *New World Writing*, since there must be a lot of otherwise well-informed people to whom jazz was just as incomprehensible as it was to our two friends. So here it is.

At first we talked about a sort of expanded glossary. But this approach has a serious fault. It starts in with the very thing which prevents a simple, empirical beginning, the mysterious but utterly unimportant argot of the jazz mystique. Some of the audience were hip. Some weren't. Some dug the scene. Some didn't dig. What do these terms mean? This question just distracts from the simple musical experience, the ordinary empirical event which is going on.

What is jazz? First off, it is music, not a voice of revolt, not a social mystique, a "way of life." It is music of a rather simple kind as music goes in the twentieth century, and so it should be fairly easy to define and describe. But there are almost as many answers to the question "What is jazz?" as there are jazz critics—not widely different answers, except for a few cranks, but varied, and clustered around a sort of loose consensus of definition. This is as it should be. General questions in the arts should not admit too specific answers. If you were to ask a committee of experts "What is Cubism?" or "What is Baroque music?" you would get similarly varied answers. Furthermore, take the question "What is Cubism?" If you had never seen a Cubist picture, the most expert answers would not help you to visualize a picture that had much resemblance to the real thing. The ultimate appeal in criticism is always to the direct experience of the work of art itself. So it is best first to listen attentively to the music of a first-rate jazz band or soloist. Instead of doing that, let's take the wrong way first. Take a typical list of the characteristics of jazz:

It employs dance forms, until recent years almost exclusively in 4/4 time.

Its material comes from folksong, mostly Negro and Southern white, religious, secular, and work songs, especially the spiritual and the Negro blues.

It usually has a limited and very characteristic harmonic and melodic structure which it shares with blues and spirituals.

Its rhythmic devices are derived from the same sources and from earlier band music.

Melody, rhythm, dynamics, ornamentation, tone color, sonority—all owe a great deal to imitation of the human voice.

21

Although some jazz was written out, even in the earliest days, and most that gets to records is at least "arranged," almost all jazz leaves a great deal of freedom for improvisation.

Six points on which practically all critics would agree. There is only one trouble. If you drop the words Negro (blues-spirituals) and substitute French or German, all six apply equally well to the music of Couperin or Bach. Does this mean that the essence of the question is the Negro origin of jazz or that something has been omitted in our definition? Perhaps it would be best to start over and listen to some music first. Here are three moderately unrare old 78's that have, in their separate ways, long been favorites of mine:

Myra Hess, *Gigue from the Fifth French Suite*, Columbia, D 1635
Jelly Roll Morton, *Tom Cat Blues*, Gennett, 5515B
Theolonius Monk, *Ruby, My Dear*, Blue Note, 549.

Is there any immediate and obvious difference? I think there is, one that no one could possibly miss. They all have, in different ways and to different degrees, something that was left out in our six points. (It so happens that they do meet, in addition, all six requirements too.) They swing. But they swing in different ways and each, in order, swings more than the one before. What is this swing? Listen again. It is an organic, flexible, fluctuating (one could go on adding adjectives of the same sort) treatment of the rhythms of a fairly simple dance form.

Contrast these, including the Myra Hess, with any readily available reading of the Beethoven *Contradances*. They don't swing at all, although they are based directly, at first hand, on German folk dance music. Back in the days of the "Swing Craze" and Maxine Sullivan's *It Was a Lover and His Lass*, and Benny Goodman's *Mr. Bach Goes to Town*, it was common to "swing the classics." Probably it could be done with the *Contradances*, but they are extraordinarily resistant to such treatment. Like doggerel in poetry, in German folk material as reworked by the composers of the Classical and Romantic periods, all the rhythmic elements tend to coincide. Accent, beat, time division, phrasing, all fall on the same notes, which gives that easily recognized Staten Island Ferry, *Ach Du Lieber Augustin, Where Oh Where Has Mine Leedle Dog Gone?*, mechanical jump to so much of Beethoven, Schubert, Schumann, and the rest, and to the playing of Baroque composers by musicians who knew only the methods of the nineteenth century. By the time we get to Liszt's *Mephisto Waltz*, any sort of natural rhythm has vanished altogether.

Although Myra Hess was certainly one of the freest interpreters of Bach—she had a peculiar *art nouveau* rhythm that makes Bach sound like Debussy—she sounds incomparably more rigid than Morton, let alone Monk. What is this swing? It is always treated as a great mystery by critics who don't play music and by jazz musicians for whom it is a valuable trade secret. It is a pretty simple secret. It is, of

23

course, the organic rhythm with which the music is executed. Jazz is played music, it is never written music. Improvised or not, its essence lies in the shared spontaneity of performer and audience. Take the most expert musicological transcription—changing time signatures, triple dotted eighth notes, asterisks above quarter tones and all the rest—give it to conventional musicians who have never heard jazz, and it won't come out jazz.

Taking the long and wide view of all the world's music, there is nothing new or strange about organic rhythm. It is the Western music of the past few hundred years that is new and strange. It was only in the eighteenth century that rigorous interpretation of our method of scoring became common and eventually universal. Few people who listen to music are aware that our musical notation dates back only to the early Renaissance and that at first it was looked on only as an approximation, a kind of shorthand to be interpreted with great freedom. Oswald Spengler had the ingenious idea that the rigorous equivalence of time in Western music from 1700 to 1900 went with the dominance of Newton's physics. Maybe he had something. To write music at all, it must be schematized and made mechanical. To play it as written reduced it to a relatively few simple elements. Given the same metronome beat, one measure is interchangeable with any other in the same time signature and key. This has led some critics, or rather musical aestheticians, to compare the fluent rhythms of "ethnic," pre-Bach, modernist, and jazz music to Bergson's organic time

24

—as contrasted with the classical time of strictly ticking exactly equivalent instants.

There is really no need to turn to philosophy. All we need to do is listen to the records of acknowledged skilled interpreters. Take the simplest possible rhythm, Dave Tough giving the beat to Jack Teagarden in *Swinging on the Teagarden Gate*, Columbia 35323. If this was transcribed, it would just be "Thump, thump; thump, thump." Anybody could do it, a metronome would do just as well. But Dave Tough is not considered by many critics to be one of the few really great musicians in jazz for nothing. (Almost all of his work is, if scored, rhythmically very simple. Although he made the transition from traditional to modern jazz, he died before he was able to develop a full modern style and it is in his simplest period that he is greatest.) Those thumps are not the blows of a machine, but echoes and variations of the human pulse; each thump is special and unique, and like a heart beat, never to be repeated.

So the larger units of rhythmic pattern are referable to other activities of the living, functioning human body, singly, in pairs, in groups. Thus the elementary phrase or cadence reflects and varies the ebb and flow of the breath. Sometimes, in certain folksongs, it is a specific kind of work—the capstan walk of the chanty, hammer drive songs like *John Henry*, or *As I Walked Out in the Streets of Laredo* or *I Ride An Old Paint*—which are rhythmically right only when they recall the motion of a night-walking horse. Anybody who has ever worked on the range knows that not only does the true cowboy ballad swing in "horse time," but that you can change the pace of your horse by changing the rhythm of your song.

In every case, the materials of natural rhythm continually vary. This does not mean after the fashion of the scored or indicated variations of a set rhythm—rubato, anticipation, suspension, syncopation, and so on, but in essence and by nature, as each step or motion of the hand is different from every other. Of course the typical expression of the union of music and the human body is the dance. Although now it is fashionable to listen and not to dance, jazz is first and foremost dance music.

Dance music enters us, becomes part of us, more than most other kinds, but music as such is the most kinesthetic of all the arts. Sound seems to take place inside, sight we think of as "out there." So we manipulate by sight and touch, we communicate by sound. "Jazz," of course, whatever the square etymologists may say, originally meant sexual intercourse, as either noun or verb, and still is immediately understood by almost anyone in America if used in that sense. And jazz, the music, grew up with dancing that was felt to be extremely erotic.

Curiously, for the past 150 years every new foreign importation into first popular and then symphonic music has been felt to be especially sexy. Music critics, like bad poets with imprecise vocabularies, have practically made the equation exotic = erotic. Tolstoy, as is well known, thought there was something very lewd about *The Kreutzer Sonata* and equated it with the dangers of canoeing and primitive sweater girls. Conversely, in the West, the folk material of Tchaikovsky was considered aphrodisiac. Polish dance patterns in Chopin, Russian folk music from Moussorgsky to the early Stravinsky, even the artificial exoticism of Debussy with its limp, *art nouveau* lassitude, every new rhythm has been rejected with the same censure, or, by the more sophisticated, welcomed with the same approval. To this day the French, more than any other people, go into raptures over Wagner, whose turgid, beery eroticism is so utterly foreign to the *clarté* and wit of the French boudoir. He still seems to send the audience of the Opéra like Katherine Dunham used to send the early audiences of Café Society Downtown. The entire history of the introduction of new folk material into the armamentarium of cultivated music is the story of the slow sublimation or etherealization of what was originally felt by the more conventional to be purely pornographic musical composition. Early nineteenth-century tirades against the waltz or the mazurka are almost incomprehensible today. Is this, and only this, what goes on in the social acceptance of jazz?

I think not. Most jazz critics are primarily discographers. They are anxious to present jazz as "pure music" for listening, in concerts or in small jazz night clubs with no dance floors. Nobody ever says that Kenton, Herman, let alone Basie, make most of their money—not by playing for Norman Grantz's Jazz at the Philharmonic—but playing dance dates at the Elks' Club in Dallas and such like places. Presumably they have never been to such dances. I suddenly realized that if I am not careful in this article I will be

27

lending myself to this ignorance or this hoax. After all, I was there. I danced at 63rd and Cottage in the Twenties in Merry Gardens, Midway Gardens, the Trianon, over on State Street in the Sunset, the Dreamland, the Fiume, at Ike Bloom's Midnight Frolics, over West at Marigold Gardens. I knew the musicians, the girls in the chorus line. I can assure you that we used to dance stuck together like postage stamps and squirming like electrocuted limpets. The dancing of the Jazz Age was as close to public copulation as you could get without being arrested. As a matter of fact, every Saturday night lots of people did get arrested, or at least put off the dance floor.

Why pretend differently? That famous article in a bygone *Etude* that all the jazz historians quote as a scandalous misunderstanding of jazz is perfectly correct as to facts. The only answer is not denial but "So, what's the matter with it?" Until this is admitted, discussions of the essence of jazz are going to get nowhere. Jazz is dance music. It is exceptionally erotic dance music, and in its evolution it has always been subject to the demands of a powerful pressure group—the people who spend the money—the dance lobby.

Does anybody ever listen? "Jelly roll," and still earlier and more folkloristic, "hog-eye" are both euphemisms for the female pudendum. Here are two titles, pulled at random from my collection: Georgia White, "Let My Love Come Down," and "Strewin' Your Mess." How about the words of a song like "Spike Driver," or "If You Want It, You Got to Buy It, 'Cause I Ain't Givin' Nothin' Away"? How about the "dirty dozens," any verse of which would

28

make this publication unmailable? I went to rent parties where Jimmy Yancey played. What is the commonest boogie-woogie verse? "Boogie to the left, boogie to the right, when I get to boogying, gonna boogie all night./Boogie down the hall, boogie out the door, when I can't stand no more, we boogie on the floor." I ask you!

Now it is true that, just like the waltz or the mazurka, the dance forms of jazz have tended, in the hands of some musicians, to grow more and more etherealized. Also, and perhaps more important, it seems that the aphrodisiac effects of all but the most obvious music tend to wear out. Could it be that the rhythms of the source activity itself change? Certainly *The Merry Widow Waltz* no longer arouses the passions as it did at the beginning of the century—even so late as John Gilbert and Mae Murray.

To many people traditional jazz doesn't sound "hot" at all but like merry-go-round music. But jazz certainly still has its roots in erotic dance and the further it gets away from these roots the less jazzy it becomes, the more it loses the distinguishing jazz "swing." It is the specific dance forms which also, in the first instance, distinguish different kinds of jazz. It is the way people responded that made the initial difference. The kind of smooth, sophisticated, satiny rhythm which we think of today as especially Ellington's first came into public notice with the dance revolution led by Vernon and Irene Castle. And who was the Castles' band leader? Jim Europe—with James P. Johnson, Eubie Blake, Willie the Lion Smith, a founder of the Clef Club—the first place where people like Huneker, Ben de Casseres, Paul

Rosenfeld, Carl Van Vechten used to go, hold their heads in their hands, and make like *Die Kunst der Fuge*—long before a single *Club Hot* had appeared in France. The Castles invented a silky, slinky elegance that has never died out. Perhaps they reflected the first awakening of a barbarous land to the possibilities of relaxed, conscious, erotic control. Who can say? Certainly the motions of the human body—any part of it—governed by Kid Ory's *Muskrat Ramble* are far more direct and instinctive. Jim Europe never recorded any jazz, as Buddy Bolden never recorded anything, and so he is just a legend.

Early jazz from the middle states of the Mississippi Valley also shows strong traces of its origins in local styles. The stomp and sand-shuffle still to this day linger in the characteristic Kansas City swing—still throbbing in the music of the latest Count Basie band, and giving a distinct rhythmic sense to all of his important former side men, however far they may have wandered from the original Moten-Kirk-Basie style. Listen to any record of the Basie band and notice how easy it is to isolate the guitar-bass-piano—the living voice of a thousand bygone blues guitarists of the old Southwest.

Recently there has been a sort of revolt against the "New Orleans Myth" of the origin of jazz—a revolt led by Leonard Feather. Duke Ellington shocked many old jazz buffs by saying that Jelly Roll Morton wasn't as good as many piano teachers around Baltimore and Washington in the early days. I think they have something. Jazz wasn't invented in New Orleans, but it wasn't invented by the

30

Jenkin's Orphanage Band in Charleston, either, or by W. C. Handy in Memphis. Dozens of local schools and styles, hundreds of anonymous musicians all over the country from Oklahoma to New York helped to form the jazz that came into public notice in the Caucasian world just prior to the first World War. To a certain extent it is still possible to sort out some of these strains by studying the more "ethnic" folk music of the countryside—country blues, ring shouts, worksongs, wandering primitive guitarists and piano players—all of whom have been recorded extensively.

New Orleans did contribute certain definite things. In the first place, the dispossession of the well-to-do colored families, many of them educated in Paris and unusually cultured for Southerners, and the driving of them into the Negro ghetto which took place towards the end of the century with the wrecking of all the benefits of Reconstruction —this forced mixing of two vital but disparate cultural groups led to a kind of explosion in the Negro community. It was not that they had more white blood, it was that they had more French civilization. "All my folks was Frenchmens," says Jelly Roll Morton rather pathetically. It is a commonplace of history that such forced mixtures usually lead to considerable social and artistic activity. Another thing—it is curious that the only two peoples in the Western world with a strong popular tradition of the prostitute's song, which is what the "city blues" is, are the French and the American Negroes. Germaine Montero singing *Rodeuse de Berges*, Edith Piaf singing *L'Autre Coté de la Rue*—

31

take away the folksong background that shaped the specifically musical idiom and what is the difference between them and hundreds of blues? There existed, at the end of the nineteenth century, and still persists in a weakened condition today, an entertainment business circuit, including everything from prostitution to opera, throughout the French colonial and former colonial world. I would not be so bold as to say that the *café chantant* had a direct influence in New Orleans, but no one else has ever suggested it and it is worth a thought.

The sources of a local style or a whole period may not be purely "folk" at all. James Reese Europe, Noble Sissle, Eubie Blake, James P. Johnson, Fletcher Henderson, Duke Ellington—somewhere along this line "commercial dance music" stops and a definite New York style emerges in jazz. The rather commercial, square, even Uncle Tom, greatest-of-all Negro revues, *Shuffle Along*, is still reverberating in jazz history.

Rhythmic and melodic patterns, even certain social attitudes (the High Society Glide versus boogie-woogie) vary with the folksong background and the demands of the dancing audience, but the kind of rhythm remains the same. The sprung rhythms, jumped beats, 5-, 7-, or 9-beat recurring accents can be found in a Gullah ringshout or, as a matter of fact, even in the preaching techniques of certain famous storefront or peasant preachers. Nobody has ever proved the blue scale, the flatted third and seventh, a bona fide African importation. Jazz buffs are infuriated by the suggestion that it might be the Dorian mode, the scale in D on the white keys. But the most popular Southern hillbilly and old Scotch and English folksong scale is the Dorian mode, and many blues—for instance, *Careless Love,* are simply Negro renditions of white Southern Dorian folksongs. Of course the "altered" notes are imprecise, but so are they in white folksong, and still, they certainly can't be when played on the piano, whatever the player's color.

Whatever the origin of the scale, this similarity made it very easy for tunes to be assimilated by Negro singers. *Careless Love* demonstrably did not come from Dahomey. So, too, with rhythmic patterns. Polkas and schottisches, let alone ragtime, can still be heard in the background of the earliest jazz pianists—even, I believe, the special grace notes and riffs of the French low life piano and accordion from urban sources and French Cajun material from the country.

In passing—ragtime is not jazz, although it is possible to "jazz" ragtime. Scott Joplin playing *Maple Leaf Rag* recorded from a piano roll sounds very mechanical compared with even the earliest jazz piano. This is not due, as most people seem to think, to the mechanical piano; actually a good player piano can transmit quite a range of dynamic subtleties. That is the way ragtime pianists wanted it. The whole point is the smooth efficiency, the precision with which syncopation, suspension, anticipation, is managed and the sharp definition of ornamentation, glissandos, and tremolos. As W. C. Handy says, "Ragtime was played as written." And some of it was anything but "primitive piano." Scott Joplin's *School of Ragtime,* his book of

33

études, could well be restored to the modern jazz repertory. The pieces should be quite spectacular in the hands of
a real swinging pianist. Jelly Roll Morton has a long discussion with Lomax about how the ragtimers played ragtime and how he played it. The whole thing is a question
of organic rhythm—the specifically jazz "swing"—and
of course, behind that, the demands of Jelly Roll's dance
audience, who wanted a more erotic style of dancing. Fats
Waller covers the whole field—there are Waller rolls
which are pure ragtime, others which start the development
toward jazz, and records which cover the whole rhythmic
gamut, ragtime, show tunes, jazz, night-club music, sentimental ballad accompaniments, cocktail piano. If Mary
Lou Williams had been recorded as early in her life and
as much, we would have an even more extensive coverage,
stretching down to the modern, post-bop period. Nothing
pays better than the study of one artist, like Mary Lou, or
Duke, or Tough, or Basie, whose work has kept alive to
changing styles and grown through the years. You can sit
down and give yourself a chronological record concert
which will pretty well answer the question "What is jazz?"

The folk material flows in, the dance figures go by—
Bunny Hug, Castle Walk, Hesitation (producing a very
erotic lyric for *Hesitation Blues* which remained the standard "dirty dozen" chorus for years), tangos, Boston, Lindy
Hop, various fox trots, the cakewalk, the Charleston, the
Shimmy (originally the Shimmy Shewabble, a shake dance
of African origin), the Black Bottom, and, with the swing
era, the return of open dancing and elaborately patterned

steps, the jitterbug revolution and the accompanying break-through of the music into new rhythmic complexities. For many years the only white dancing that resembled the open dramatic dancing that came in with the swing period was that of Joe Frisco, first called "The American Apache," later billed as "The Jazz Dancer," a perennial favorite of the Orpheum Circuit and Ziegfeld's *Follies*. The more sophisticated youngsters of the Twenties idolized him, and an imitation of his routines was sure to get you thrown off the dance floor, even of Merry Gardens or the toughest South State Street joint . . . as would, for that matter, a good hot Valentino tango. Frisco had quite a tango of his own—the first "air steps" I ever saw, and, alas, could never imitate successfully! (When I think of the innocent girls that risked their lovely necks in these capers!) Frisco claimed to be the first white entertainer to put a jazz band in Palace Time—Jimmy Durante must have run him a close second. It was the dancing, not the music that attracted the most censure in the Jazz Age. Criticism of the music could not have been more wrong. "Shrieking discords," "insane rhythms," back in the days when what was most characteristic of jazz was its rhythmic simplicity—4/4 time—and its elementary harmony—the use of only a few basic chords. It was the erotic pulse of the rhythm, the swing, and not the strangeness nor the complexity, that the editorial writers and preachers objected to, just as they had objected to *Dance du Ventre Polka, The Authentic Coochi Coochi as danced by Little Egypt*. Jazz was a music of re-

35

volt—but it was the music of revolt against Puritanism, not against Capitalism.

Nothing is more absurd than the balderdash so common amongst Crow Jim French and British critics, that jazz is "the voice of the downtrodden Negro people." True, many spirituals are practically code songs of slave protest; Miles Mark Fisher's *Negro Slave Songs in the United States* demonstrates this very cogently, and many blues singers, especially males, have scant shrift for the values of white society. The sources of jazz are influenced by racial and social conflict, but jazz itself appears first as part of the entertainment business, and the enraged proletariat do not frequent night clubs or cabarets.

One of the most ridiculous things I ever read was a description, by some French aesthete, of the old Sunset, made immortal by Armstrong, as though it was some sort of musical tempestuous Unit Meeting of the "exploited Negroes of Chicago's stockyards and steel mills." I have read similar things about the Cotton Club. Now I almost never went to the Sunset because, although I knew the owner, it cost in the neighborhood of thirty dollars to take a girl and dance or sit through a couple of sets. As for the Cotton Club —lest I be thought chauvinistic, let me quote Langston Hughes' autobiography, from his chapter entitled in bitter irony "When the Negro Was in Vogue" and which you should certainly read:

"White people began to come to Harlem in droves. For several years they packed the expensive Cotton

Club on Lenox Avenue. But I was never there, because the Cotton Club was a Jim Crow club for gangsters and moneyed whites. They were not cordial to Negro patronage unless you were a celebrity like Bojangles (Robinson)."

I have been to the Cotton Club, and let me say that in addition the acts were vulgar and chauvinistic past belief. If one of them were put on today the NAACP would have a picket line which would fill the block in front of the place. On the platform above the horrors of chorus and comics was the Ellington band, imperturbable, elegant, and infinitely contemptuous. Duke earned that famous dignity the hard way. As a matter of bitter literal fact it was cheaper to dance or listen to a white jazz band than to the more famous colored ones. I think it cost fifty cents to go to White City and enjoy the music of McPartland, Tough, Teschemacher, and Bud Freeman, and even the Coon-Saunders Band at the Blackstone was cheaper than the Sunset. Obscure gutbucket bands played places like the Fiume where only very bohemian whites ever dared to go.

The notion that jazz is social protest music is the product of the systematic anti-American paranoia of French intellectuals and the Friends of the Soviet Union folk culture of a couple of Greenwich Village night clubs of the Thirties. The protest was sexual and unconscious, practically automatic. It is simply that a natural expression of courtship, the oldest, the most anthropological function of music and dance, returned to American culture. It was part of the gen-

37

eral overthrow of the English, New England Puritan tradition and the reassertion of the powerful French and Negro elements of our culture. And it is for this reason, if any, that its central nervous system, its main arteries and veins, were the rivers of the drainage of the Mississippi, that French and Negro river.

Of course it is true that no protest is more profound and more vital than a sexual one, for the simple reason that it involves the very vitals of the members of society. So, if it meets with repression and gives rise to social conflict, as jazz certainly did and still does, it soon involves a whole overturn of all the values of conventional society. This is the source of the jazz mystique, jazz as a "way of life," the hostility to "square society" now systematized in the antics of the hipster.

The natural response to my line of argument here is "What has this got to do with modern jazz, with bop, with cool or progressive jazz, with the quiet, calm complexities of Pacific jazz, with the intricacies of the Modern Jazz Quartet or the modernist adventures of Charles Mingus?" Here the temptation is very strong to take refuge in the well-worked quotation from Lester Young, "If you have to ask, you'll never know." Can you dance to Mingus or Milt Jackson or Theolonius Monk? Well, yes, I guess you could if you had to, but that is the point. Can you dance to a Chopin waltz? What you are witnessing is the etherealization of form which takes place with all similar introductions of folk material into the mainstream of music. You can, I guess, if you want, dance to the most modern jazz, but you don't have to. The same effects are obtained by more subtle means. And unlike Hungarian music in the hands of Liszt, the jazz heritage is much more resistant. It can only be etherealized just so much. It still swings or it ceases to be jazz. Charles Mingus may sound less funky than Oscar Pettiford to the layman, but Pettiford has a trained ear. *He* recognizes the continuity. Just as you can tell the difference between a Florida orange and a California orange, there is an indisputable difference between Harlem 1958 hard bop and Pacific jazz. But it is a difference of mood, not of essence. Possibly California, with its notorious sophistication, has developed a more relaxed and imaginative sexual technique.

If jazz is music of revolt, it is a revolt towards more natural, wholesome, normal human relationships. A whole generation of novelists, not just D. H. Lawrence, drove home the point that a pig roast on Papeete is a more healthy human get-together than a literary cocktail party on Madison Avenue. This is hardly in need of laboring today. Who doubts it? Jazz returns social music to the role that it has played in all human societies from time immemorial and which was only forgotten for a brief period in Western civilization. This is why it is of such tremendous importance, why it is America's greatest contribution to twentieth-century culture, and, if not the only serious music we have, our only music which anybody outside the country takes seriously. After all, a revolution in basic human relationships is a very important revolution indeed. Just incidentally, nothing shows better the way in which the arts

39

play a social role—secretly, behind the scenes, seldom understood by the official critics of art and literature, and, eventually, totally subversive.

So to come to the jazz "mystique." Does the hipster with his green beret, black glasses, and embouchure whisker, the band rat with her Theda Bara make-up and dirty feet in Jesus sandals, the amateur dope fiends with their adulterated marijuana, the Beat Generation, do these people represent "jazz as a way of life"? God forbid! Marx said of Bakunin that he suffered from *furor aristocraticus*. The hipster is the furious square. The Beat novelists and poets and their camp followers are debauched Puritans. They agree with the most hostile critics of jazz, or for that matter with the most chauvinistic slanderers of the American Negro. They just like it that way. In their utter ignorance they embrace the false image which their enemies the squares have painted.

As Charles Mingus once said to me, "We didn't evolve the new forms of modern jazz in dirty cellars full of dope peddlers. We worked it out in people's homes, which we didn't call 'pads' either. And our families stood around and listened and approved."

Jazz musicians are entertainers and the entertainment business is terribly hard work, with awful hours and long weeks spent lonely on The Road. It is true that they relax in rather unconventional ways and keep different hours from the majority, but that gruelling experience, which everybody hates, "The Road," is a far different thing from the car-wrecking, switchblade orgy of a popular novel with the same name. It is true that Harlem is a hell of a place and warps the lives of everybody who lives there, not just of musicians. But even in Harlem, and far more so in the rest of the country, and, I suppose, most of all on the Pacific Coast, most of the musicians I know are devoted artists—interested primarily in their work, in their wives and children, and, like all of us, in the hard job of keeping a home going in spite of the conspiracy of the society in which we live to destroy it.

Norman Mailer has spoken of the hipster as an imitator of the Negro, but it is imitation characterized by total ignorance of its model. A well known Beat Poet recently told an interviewer for United Press that "Bird [Charles Parker] couldn't have blown such beautiful notes if he hadn't taken heroin." I knew Bird pretty well, and he sure as Hell didn't think so—he didn't like it at all. Possibly the Beat Poet wouldn't recognize "beautiful notes" if he heard them, and I am sure he would not know how to conduct himself if invited to dinner in the home of a jazz musician, assuming that anybody would be so foolish as to invite him. Hipsters are the parasites on the body of jazz, and the sooner they are got rid of, with a good dose of Larkspur Lotion and blue ointment, the better.

# RIMBAUD
# AS CAPITALIST
# ADVENTURER

Most people think of Rimbaud as the very archetype of
youth in revolt, as well as the founder of modernist poetry
and one of the greatest secular, that is non-religious, or in
his case anti-religious, mystics. A kind of Rimbaudian
orthodoxy has grown up which meets with very little protest. A few European critics have spoken in demurrer, but
most interested Americans have never heard of them. I
think myself that the whole Rimbaudian gospel is open to
question.

The very title of his prose poems raises this question.
Mrs. Varèse discusses some aspects in her excellent introduction.* Does it mean "illuminations," as in medieval
manuscripts? The French verb is *enluminurer*. "Illuminations" is usually considered an English import into French.
Does it mean mystical insights? Does it mean bits of illumination in the French sense—enlightenment? (This again
in the ironic French sense; an *illuminé* is very close to being a sophisticate or, feminine, a bluestocking.) Nobody
ever suggests that the first meaning to occur to an unruly
adolescent boy might be "fireworks." I vote for fireworks.

---

* *Illuminations*. By Arthur Rimbaud. Translated by Louise Varèse. New
Directions, N.Y., 1957.

The neuroses the treatment of which now consumes so much of the budget of the more fashionable members of the American upper middle class are actually, by and large, palpitations of behavior due to unsatisfied bourgeois appetites and lack of life aim. In the young, especially in the young poor, the syndrome is called delinquency. Its ravages are often attributed to television. Television has a lot to do with it all right, but not the horror serials, the Westerns, and crime shockers. The real source of corruption is the commercial. It is possible to mistake a demoralized craving for Cadillacs for "revolt." Revolutionaries hitherto have not expressed themselves by snitching the gaudier appurtenances of conspicuous expenditure. Genuine revolt goes with an all-too-definite life aim—hardly with the lack of it. Whether or not there is anything genuine about the vision, whether the visionary really sees anything, is open to dispute, but there is a wide consensus as to what the genuine experience is like, and how the genuine visionary behaves. As Baron von Hugel pointed out in one of his most penetrating observations, true illumination always results in a special sweetness of temper, a deep, lyric equanimity and magnanimity. The outstanding characteristic of the mystic's vision is that it is satisfying. He is never frustrated, at least not in our worldly sense. It would be hard to find two less suitable words in any language to apply to Rimbaud than equanimity and magnanimity. This leaves us with Rimbaud as a sort of magician of the sensibility—of that specifically modern sensibility invented by Blake and Hoelderlin and Baudelaire—and an innovator in syntax,

43

the first thoroughly radical revealer of the poetic metalogic which is the universal characteristic of twentieth-century verse.

I think this is enough. I don't think anybody has ever demonstrated convincingly that behind the syntactic surface lay the profound content of a sort of combination Bakunin and St. John of the Cross. The content is the season in hell, the dark night of the soul, the struggle with God and the State, of all adolescence. This, of course, has its own common profundity. I do not doubt but what the first flares to burn in the gonads of puberty do light up the ultimate questions of the fate and meaning of man, but that is not what the Rimbaudians mean. The excitement and fury is not metaphysical, it is youthful. The cocksureness is youthful too, but it is also something else. It is bourgeois. Rimbaud did not lose himself in Africa; he found himself. The average poet turns to writing because he can't compete with his schoolmates in track and football. High school dances frighten him. He never learns the proper passes that score with a chick in the back seat of a convertible. In fact, he never gets near one. But there are always a few girls, not very appetizing, most of them, who will be nice to a fellow who has made "The Lit." So, he invests in a set of Dowson, Housman, and T. S. Eliot and starts in. This was not Rimbaud's approach. He applied to literature, and to litterateurs, the minute he laid eyes on them, the devastating methods of total exploitation described so graphically in the *Communist Manifesto*. Some of them were not very applicable. He "ran" the vowels like he later ran guns to

44

the Abyssinians, with dubious results. Usually, however, he was very successful—in the same way his contemporaries Jim Fiske and P. T. Barnum were successful. He did things to literature that had never been done to it before, and they were things which literature badly needed done to it . . . just like the world needed the railroads the Robber Barons did manage to provide.

Not for nothing is *Bateau Ivre* a schoolboy's dream of Cowboys and Indians—that's where Rimbaud belonged, on the frontier—with Cecil Rhodes. And that is where, back in his home town, he was immortalized. The old monument to Rimbaud in Charleville ignores his poetry and memorializes him as the local boy who made good as a merchant and hero of French imperialism in the Africa where the aesthetes who were never good at business think he went to die unknown, holding the Ultimate Mystery at bay.

# THE VISIONARY
# PAINTING OF
# MORRIS GRAVES

It is not well known around the world that there existed in the nineteenth-century United States a very considerable visionary art. William Blake and his disciples, Samuel Palmer and Edward Calvert, Francis Danby and John Martin, the later Turner, the Pre-Raphaelites, Odilon Redon, Gustave Moreau, the Nabis, were popular in America and had considerable influence. Most of the painters of this tendency are now forgotten, but one, Albert Pinkham Ryder (1847–1917), has survived in popular esteem as one of America's greatest artists. In our own time visionary painting has been at a discount all over the world, in spite of some interest stirred up a generation ago by the Surrealists, but it is quite possible that the re-evaluation which has brought back Palmer, Calvert, and Redon, may in time to come restore many more forgotten reputations, even Moreau, who, say what you will, is the master of Rouault at least.

It is to this tendency of American painting that Morris Graves belongs. However, he is beyond question a richer and more skillful artist than any of his predecessors, and, to put it simply, a better, "greater" painter than any of them, except possibly Ryder. In recent years a whole new school of American painting, abstract-expressionism, has come to maturity and begun to influence painting around the world. Painters such as Rothko, Still, Pollock, Motherwell, de Kooning, and Ferren now seem to be the forerunners of what may be the international style of the coming decade. Morris Graves, however, stands apart from the expressionist group, as, at the other extreme of contemporary style, does a figure of comparable stature, Ben Shahn.

Morris Graves is less provincial, far more a "citizen of the world" than any of his predecessors of the visionary school. It is curious to reflect on this fact, a symptom of the terrific acceleration of the civilizing process of this continent, for Graves was born, raised, and came to maturity as an artist in the Pacific Northwest, a region that was a wilderness until the last years of the nineteenth century. Greatly as I admire Graves's work, it must be admitted that certain of its characteristics are those found, not at the beginning, but at the end of a cultural process—hypersensitivity, specialization of subject, extreme refinement of technique. Nothing could show better the essentially world-wide, homogeneous nature of modern culture than that this successor to the great Sung painters sprang up in a region that was created out of a jungle-like rain forest by the backwash of the Alaska gold rush.

People in the rest of the United States and in Europe have difficulty in adjusting to the fact that the Pacific Coast of America faces the Far East, culturally as well as geographically. There is nothing cultish about this, as there might be elsewhere. The residents of California, Oregon,

47

and Washington are as likely to travel across the Pacific as across the continent and the Atlantic. Knowledge of the Oriental languages is fairly widespread. The museums of the region all have extensive collections of Chinese, Japanese, and Indian art. Vedantist and Buddhist temples are to be seen in the coast cities. And of course there are large Chinese and Japanese colonies in every city, and proportionately even more Orientals in the countryside. It is interesting to note that besides the direct influence of the Orient on them, the Seattle painters, Graves, Tobey, and Callahan, the Portland painter, Price, the San Francisco abstract-expressionists, have all avoided the architectural limited-space painting characteristic of Western Europe from the Renaissance to Cubism, and show more affinity to the space concepts of the Venetians. Venice, of course, was for centuries Europe's chief window on the East, an enclave of Byzantine civilization, and the first contact with China. There are drawings by Tintoretto that might have been done in his contemporary China. I do not believe that this has been a conscious influence in most cases, but rather an example of what anthropologists call convergence.

Graves was born in 1910 in the Fox Valley of Oregon and has lived in the state of Washington, in or near Seattle, all his life, except for short visits to Japan in 1930, to the Virgin Islands in 1939, to Honolulu in 1947, and a year in Europe in 1948, after his personal style was fully developed and "set." He studied at the Seattle Museum, with the old master of Northwest painting, Mark Tobey, and had his first one-man show there in 1936. His first New York

shows were in 1942 at the Willard Gallery and the Museum
of Modern Art. His paintings are now to be found in the
permanent collections of most of the major American museums, including the Metropolitan in New York.

Except for the emphasis on deep complex space and
calligraphic skill which he learned from Tobey, but which
he could just as well have learned from the Far Eastern
paintings in the Seattle Museum, Graves's style, or styles,
his special mode of seeing reality and his techniques of
handling it, have come, like the spider's web, out of himself, or, at the most, out of the general cultural ambience
of a world civilization, syncretic of all time and space.
Therefore, influences and resemblances which seem certain
to a historian of art may never in actual fact have existed.
Since today Graves's painting is an extremely specialized
view of reality and his concept of space differs from that
usually thought of as the contribution of modern painting,
it is fruitful to compare him in his development with other
painters of other times around the world, always realizing
that, with the exception of Chinese, specifically Sung, and
Japanese, specifically Ashikaga, and particularly the
painter Sesshu, Graves himself may never have known of
any resemblance let alone influence.

The first of Graves's paintings after his apprentice days
are in a rather thick medium, often laid in like cloisonné
between broad, abrupt, dark, single brush strokes. The
colors are all "local." There is no attempt to achieve deep
space or movement in space by juxtaposition of color. In
fact the color is limited to a small gamut of earths, dull

49

reds, browns, and yellows, with occasionally a slate blue. The line, however, has a great deal of snap, while the movement is very shallow, almost Egyptian. If there are receding planes in these pictures, they are kept to a minimum and the lines stick to the silhouette, never crossing from plane to plane to fill the space. The thing that identifies these paintings immediately is a peculiar, individual sense of silhouette, a silhouette defined by an eccentric calligraphic stroke.

As is well known, a highly personal line of this type comes late, if at all, to most artists. Yet it seems to have been the first thing Graves developed. I can think of nothing quite like it. The brush drawings of the early Jean de Bosschere—not the commercial book illustrations but rather those for his own *Portes Fermées*—have somewhat the same feeling. I rather doubt that Graves has ever seen these.

This is also somewhat the style of the earliest Klees. It is generally identified with the magazine *Simplicimuss*, a German satirical publication of the years before the First War. Graves, very likely, has never heard of it.

Already in this period, which incidentally was roughly that of the WPA Art Project (1935–42), Graves was beginning to concentrate on birds and sometimes small animals as masks of man and as symbols of the personae, the forces, operating in man—a kind of transcendental Aesop.

Certainly the best picture of this period is a large *Game Cock* (1933), many times life size, caught in a thick perimeter that whips across the picture plane like jagged

50

lightning. There is no sign of the easy line so attractive to young artists who are beginning to pay attention to their drawing—the decorative sweeps of Beardsley, Botticelli, or the Book of Kells, those perennial favorites of the innocent. Neither is there any of the impressionist line of the Rodin water colors, the other and great influence on the young—and on Matisse and his descendants. This line is tooled to the last millimeter and, with the exception of the Bosscheres I spoke of, there is nothing like it except certain painted ceramics, Greek and Oriental, some Romanesque illumination, and the akimbo linearity of the Moissac Portal. It is simply not a line usually found in painting. Later this cock was to be repainted, smaller, more compact and secretive, in the two *Game Cocks* of 1939.

In his early twenties Graves had begun to concentrate on calligraphy, under the influence of Mark Tobey's "white writing," which Tobey himself was just then beginning. Graves shared practically on equal terms with the older man in its development.

At this time too Graves took a short trip to Japan and later traveled in the eastern United States and the Caribbean. The paintings of this period parallel—they cannot really be said to be influenced by—the major paintings of Tintoretto in the treatment of the picture space as a saturated manifold quivering with three-dimensional lines, really tracks of force. The best analogy is to the whorls of iron filings in a magnetic field. But in this case the field is both three dimensional and possessed of more than two poles, and all of varying intensity. This space concept reaches its highest development only in the Venetian baroque in the West, but of course it is basic in the greatest periods of Sung and Ashikaga ink painting.

In writing of Sesshu, I have said, "The brush, which never departs from the calligraphy of the square Chinese characters, is as quick, precise, powerful, and yet effortless as Japanese sword play. 'The sword,' say the Zen fencing masters, 'finds channels opened for it in space, and follows them without exertion to the wound.' This is the central plastic conception of Sesshu. The picture space is thought of as a field of tangled forces, a complex dynamic web. The brush strokes flow naturally in this medium, defining it by their own tensions, like fish in a whirlpool of perfectly clear water."

Both Tobey and Graves can be considered as direct descendants of Sesshu. In Graves there is an additional factor, a deliberate formal mysteriousness, a conscious seeking for uncanny form, analogous to that found in primitive cult objects—sacred stones and similar things. There are several series of studies of just such objects—stones and driftwood—notably the nine water colors of 1937 called *Purification*.

From 1939 to 1942 were the years of the *Little Known Bird of the Inner Eye*, *Bird in Moonlight*, and *Blind Bird*, now in the New York Museum of Modern Art collection, paintings which achieved an instantaneous fame when they were first exhibited. Every critic seems to have been aware that here was a really different yet thoroughly competent artist.

Incidentally, the haunted, uncanny character of these pictures, which reaches its height, representationally at least, in *Young Rabbit and Foxfire* and *Bird with Possessions* of 1942, owes little or nothing to Surrealism. There is much more conscious knowledge of mystery, and much less unconscious Freudian or Jungian symbolism.

On into the war years the mastery of calligraphy developed, until finally the line, sometimes "white writing," sometimes black, reaches a climax in the *Joyous Young Pine* series of 1944, *Black Waves* (1944), *In the Air* (1943), and the two great ideographs called *Waning Moon* (1943), in the Seattle Art Museum. These paintings are fully the equal of anything, East or West, of the kind. *Waning Moon* passes out of the realm of ordinary painting altogether and can be compared only with the ominous, cryptic characters which Shingon monks write on six-foot sheets of paper while in trance.

To 1945 belongs the series called *Consciousness Assuming the Form of a Crane*. I own what I consider the best of these, and for nine years I have found its ephemeral simplicity inexhaustible. In these paintings the old dynamic hyperactive space of Sesshu has been surpassed. The background is a vague cloudy diagonal drift of red and green, overcast with a frost of white. From this, in a few faint strokes of white with touches of somber red, emerges a slowly pacing, more than life-size crane-being rising from flux into consciousness, but still withdrawn, irresponsible, and stately. There is nothing exactly like this in the world's art, for it is not simply a literary or a mystical notion but a

53

plastic one as well. Form, an ominous, indifferent form, emerges from formlessness, literally seems to bleed quietly into being.

The great dragon painters of the Orient whose dragons are confused with and only half emerge from vortexes of clouds and rain were seeking the same kind of effect, but of course their paintings are far more active. Graves's *Cranes* are not active at all. They are as quiet as some half-caught telepathic message.

In 1948, Graves traveled in Europe. Much of this time was spent at Chartres. Just before leaving America he had done a series of what can only be described as intensely personal portraits of Chinese Shang and Chou bronzes. Objects of great mystery in their own right, in Graves's paintings they become visions, supernatural judgments of the natural world. *Individual State of the World,* with its use of Graves's recurrent minnow, symbol of the spark of spiritual illumination, is representative of this series. Contemporary with these bronzes is a series of vajras (Buddhist ritual bronze thunderbolts), lotuses, and diamonds of light which can be considered as illustrations for that great refusal to affirm either being or non-being, the *Prajnaparamita Sutra.*

No one has seen what Graves did at Chartres. In conversation he has told me how he spent the better part of a cold foggy winter there, painting every day, details of the cathedral, fragments of statues, bits of lichened masonry, and several pictures of the interior of the cathedral in early morning—the great vault, half filled with thick fog, dawn beginning to sparkle in the windows. When he came back to America and reviewed the year's work he destroyed it all. I have a feeling that the painting in the Fredericks collection, *Ever Cycling*, may have survived from this time.

Shortly after this, Graves abandoned ink, gouache, and water color on paper, and returned to oil. From 1950 to the present [1955], most of the paintings are in the vein of *Guardian*—or the *Spirit Bird Transporting Minnow from Stream to Stream* of the Metropolitan collection—geese, hawks, and eagles, most of them over life size, many with mystifying accessories such as black suns or golden antlers. It would seem, looking at a sizable collection of these recent paintings, that Graves has, at least temporarily, abandoned the surcharged, dynamic, baroque space of the calligraphic paintings and returned to the intact object. Again, there is considerable resemblance to the bird painters of the Far East—the famous pair of ducks of the Sung Dynasty in the British Museum, or the early falcon painters of the Kano school. These new paintings share with them a concentration on maximum surface tension, a sense of absolutely full occupation of their separate volume, like formed globules of quicksilver, or drops of viscid oil. This particular formal quality does have a parallel in contemporary art, notably in Brancusi's sculpture of a *Fish* and those dreaming ovoids he calls *Birth*, and more especially in the most successful of Hans Arp's swollen, amoeboid figures. Piero della Francesca, of course, is the outstanding example of what might be called overloaded volume in the Renaissance. This, by the way, is a quality that must be distinguished from Picasso's excessive specific gravity—in his case a directly representational device masquerading as "significant form." Picasso and most of his disciples simply paint things to look many times as heavy as they actually are. In Graves's recent work there is always a sense of ominous, impending meaning, as if these human-eyed birds were judging the spectator, rather than he them, and in terms of a set of values incomprehensible to our sensual world.

It is none too easy to sum up such an accomplishment as that of Graves. Certainly he is one of the greatest calligraphers of all time—not just a "master of line" but a creator of significant ideographs and, beyond that, a creator of a new and strange significance of the ideograph as well. Graves has also been one of the many around the world who in this generation have freed painting from the exhausted plasticism, the concentration on architecture alone, which formed the residue of subsiding Cubism. This he has accomplished not merely, or even primarily, by illustrative, but by plastic means, by discovering a new world of form antipodal to the Poussin rigor of Cubism. Graves has opened the plastic arts to a whole range of experience hardly found in the external world at all, let alone in art. He has created a series of objects, masks, personae, which act both as objects of contemplation, and, in contemplation, as sources of values which judge the world the spectator brings to them. On the whole this judgment has little room or time for those values known to the popular mind as "American," but which are really those of our acquisitive mass Western civilization.

Jacques Maritain asks somewhere, "What kept Europe alive for so long after it had obviously been stricken with a fatal disease?" and answers his question, "The prayers of the contemplatives in the monasteries." I am not prepared to enter into a metaphysical defense of petitionary prayer, or a sociological one of monasticism, but the empirical evidence for the social, perhaps even biological necessity for contemplation, is, in these apocalyptic hours, all too obvious. Civilizations endure as long as, somewhere, they can hold life in total vision. The function of the contemplative is contemplation. The function of the artist is the revelation of reality in process, permanence in change, the place of value in a world of facts. His duty is to keep open the channels of contemplation and to discover new ones. His role is purely revelatory. He can bring men to the springs of the good, the true, and the beautiful, but he cannot make them drink. The activities of men endure and have meaning as long as they emanate from a core of transcendental calm. The contemplative, the mystic, assuming moral responsibility for the distracted, tries to keep his gaze fixed on that core. The artist uses the materials of the world to direct men's attention back to it. When it is lost sight of, society perishes.

Although the mystique behind such evaluation is overtly Oriental, even Buddhist or Vedantist, and hence anti-humanistic, I do not feel that this type of explication is really relevant. The perfected mystic, of course, would not seek to express himself at all. In the last analysis it is the artist, the contemplator and fabricator, who speaks and judges through these embodied visions. And the united act of contemplation and shaping of reality is in its essence the truest and fullest human deed. Morris Graves has said of his own work: "If the paintings are confounding to anyone—then I feel that words (my words, almost anyone's words) would add confusion. For the one to whom the message is clear or even partially clear or challengingly obscure—then, for them, words are obviously excessive. To the one whose searching is not similar to ours—or those who do not feel the awful frustrations of being caught in our individual and collective projection of our civilization's extremity—to those who believe that our extroverted civilization is constructively progressing—those who seeing and tasting the fruits and new buds of self-destructive progress are still calling it good, to them the ideas in the paintings are still preposterous, hence not worth consideration."

# THE ENNOBLING
# REVULSION

Baudelaire was the greatest poet of the capitalist epoch.
Does anybody doubt this? You would have to search for a
reputable critic who would disagree today. And yet—my
God! what a wretched fellow he was. Anybody unfamiliar
with the subject would be sure the Hyslops had rigged an
invidious selection of his letters.* They haven't done so, yet
this hundred, chosen from about a thousand that survive,
not only show him in a bad light, they never, never at all,
show him in a good one. It was unlucky for Baudelaire that
his mother saved all his letters to her. He never wrote her a
decent letter and he wrote plenty. They are all dishonest. If
he is not begging her for money, he is trying to trick her
out of it by the most transparent devices and lies. He lies
about his business affairs. He lies about his love affairs.
Always he picks at the scabs of his ulcerating oedipus complex. It is all very disgusting.

His letters to his friends are mostly concerned with literary log-rolling and wire-pulling. Again and again he
wheedles Sainte-Beuve. Again and again he is snubbed.
Precisely because he was the kind of man his letters reveal
him to be, he was not the sort that Sainte-Beuve, that slightly

---

* *Baudelaire, a Self Portrait.* Selected Letters, translated and edited with commentary by Lois Boe Hyslop and Francis E. Hyslop, Jr., Oxford University
Press.

seedy bon vivant, could take seriously. He tell his guardian he will beat him up. He stages a fake suicide. He never, not once, has a genuinely good word, never an honest one, to say for his mistress, Jeanne. At the end, she vanishes, blind, sick, and crippled. She may have been pretty bad—perverted and totally masochistic himself, Baudelaire doubtless picked quite a freak—but she put up with him for twenty years, a job which might have revolted his guardian angel. Certainly it was not for his money, because she got very little, and in her young days at least had plenty of opportunity to do better elsewhere. His love letters to other women are absurd; the scorned and beseeching lover of a tenth-rate provincial melodrama. Altogether he manages to put up an even worse front than his master, Poe.

What was great about this man? He wasn't even bad, but "delinquent," like an incorrigible, shifty, not very bright child of ten. However powerful and original his published criticism of painting and letters, in his correspondence when he writes of ideas, of literature, of art, he seldom rises above the level of a scrapbook of demoralized adolescence. Poe's *Eureka* may read like the philosophizing of Amory Blaine, but Baudelaire does not even reach these heights. It has been said that he admired Poe so much because he couldn't understand English. To judge by the letters, it was because he couldn't understand Poe. French or English, it all seemed very deep stuff to Baudelaire. Then, too, it was profitable. He seems to have made more money off his Poe translations than from anything else he did—at last to sell the entire copyright for a pittance. Why was this man one of the world's greatest writers? That is the hardest of all critical questions to answer.

In a sense it is the fundamental critical question. It must be answered just right. The slightest confusion leads to aesthetic and moral nonsense. Catullus is a great writer. Céline is a great writer. Genet is not a "writer" at all—he is a social document. Pornography is not enough. Evil living is not enough. Demoralization is not enough. Of course, everybody knows that Baudelaire was great because of the magnificence of his style. But what does this mean? Here of all places the style is the man. There is something that doesn't meet the naked eye. For the poetry to possess such grandeur, the man must have had it too. The qualities of his poetry are obvious enough to everyone but T. S. Eliot. Most of them are included in his own aesthetic of "dandyism." They are maximum tension, achieved by all sorts of means, but especially by dynamic contrasts of both style and material—the well-known use of classical rhythmic inflections in a fiercely ironic sense is a good example. Mr. Eliot took this at face value. Of course the point is that Baudelaire uses the heroic hysterics of Racine to mock his own predicament. The *Action Française* nonsense about his Catholicism is a similar error. Religion for Baudelaire is a kind of sultry farce. The Mass is a travesty of the Black Mass, rather than the other way around.

Another characteristic of Baudelaire is his overpowering gravity. Poe is always frivolous. Baudelaire is always in deadly, terrifying earnest. The *motte* of his mistress, the hallucinatory streets of Paris in the autumn evening, "lit

61

with prostitutes," the snaky hiss of taffeta petticoats, the stale sweat of poverty and lust, everything is given the life and death significance of an induced paranoia. And the verse echoes this mortal concern. Through it all beats the measuring out of ultimate crisis, the tones of his *cloche felée*. Compare them with the bell strokes of *In Memoriam* and you sense instantly the difference between the pathos of sentiment and the pathos of total tragedy.

Even so hasty a characterization makes apparent what it is that makes Baudelaire great. Homer was as professionalized as an acrobat. Butler thought Nausicaa wrote the *Odyssey*. Certainly Homer never stood on the walls of Troy beside his infant son and resolved within his own heart the ruin of all bright things. He let other men do it for him. His job was to record the acts of heroes. So too with Aeschylus and Sophocles. With the arrest of industrial and commercial civilization at the level of the French Restoration, French official culture disintegrated into a congeries of lies, like a heap of evil jackstraws. The only heroes society has to offer are confidence men. Where the poet preserves an awareness of his prophetic responsibility, where he insists that poetry still is a symbolic criticism of values, he is forced to become his own tragic hero. Society can only provide the cast for bitter comedy—Jonson's *Volpone*, Machiavelli's *Mandragola*. What is the nineteenth-century novel, from Balzac or even Choderlos de Laclos, but the representation of this malignant mockery? Anyone who pretends to mount and manage the fall of Agamemnon or the parting of Titus and Berenice in terms of the coming century and a half of revolutions betrayed is a self-con-victed fraud.

It sounds glib to say that Baudelaire embodies within himself the "contradictions of capitalism" as though he was a sort of ambulatory Falling Rate of Profit. Perhaps it can all be traced back to economics, but the tragedy of the modern world, the metaphysical horror, the Social Lie, the World Ill, these are catch phrases masking total moral breakdown, the alienation of man from his work, from his fellows, and from himself. Organized society in our epoch simply has nothing good about it. It is deadly fraud from start to finish. We are so used to it that we forget or we never face, what writers like Veblen, or Riesman, or Wright Mills mean in actual human terms.

Baudelaire or Céline face the monster all the time. They can never forget for an instant. The horrors of a world where man is wolf to man struggle all through every mo-ment in the very bloodstream, like leukemia.

Does this mean that, as the Marxists used to say, all great writers of the past two centuries have been revolutionaries, conscious or unconscious? Certainly not. Such a notion only reveals the lack of what the Russians, in signs warning you not to spit in the subway, call "culture." Léon Blum had a career and a program; Céline had a life and a work of art. Leon Trotsky said that, long ago, in the best thing he ever wrote. In the final showdown, all our revolutions have turned out to be careers for some and programs for others. The stuff of life, of art, is not only vaster far than all programs and careers, it is the material of a different qualitative world altogether.

The *Agamemnon* of Aeschylus could ennoble and purify the Greek community in ways that we can hardly realize—however well we may understand them. The hero, Baudelaire, enables us to endure a predicament we understand only too well with at least some kind of dignity. It is, in fact, a very considerable dignity, greater than can be comprehended in the term "Dandy" unless we want to give it the very special connotation he gave it—the meaning of tragic hero of the modern metropolis. But there is none of this dignity in the letters; just the terrible fires of shame out of which that dignity was forged. We can pity; but as Yeats said, the poetry is not the pity.

# MY HEAD
# GETS TOOKEN
# APART

Lawrence Lipton has a very funny poem called "I Was a Poet for the FBI." I have never precisely been a poet for them, though I doubt not but what I have caused them sufficient annoy. However, I now feel I have really made it. Fame has arrived. I have been a poet for the IPAR, formerly the OS of the OSS.

Things have been dull here beside Frisco Bay. There was a UNESCO conference. No story there, or rather, exactly the same story as the Industrial Development thing I just finished. If you want to know what happened at the UNESCO sessions, just go back to the November 2 [1957] *Nation* and put in the new names. It was the same old story. Another installment in the serial, but a little closer to the denouement. The American system of world alliances is falling apart and the only answer the lads in power have is, "If getting tough hasn't worked, get tougher." Things are tough all over this winter. We must tighten our belts and get our own dog up.

So much for UNESCO. The best thing was the show of Asian and Western art at the San Francisco Museum, which really showed a lot of fruitful cross-fertilization. It is in the world of concrete things, objects, not profits and power blocs, that the slow and painful but absolutely essential marriage of the East and West is taking place. And now that India and China and Japan produce their own nuclear physicists and astronomers, there was not even a moderately long paragraph, let alone a story. And then I got the loveliest invitation.

What a pity it can't be quoted in full, but the gist of it was that an outfit calling itself the Institute of Personality Assessment and Research, which had started out in life as the Office of Selection of the OSS, with the job of insuring that everybody in the Army brightened the corner where he were, had got a potful of gold from the Carnegie people and had transferred from the Army to that River Rouge of the intellect, the University of California, and had cut loose on the creative personality, which they were very busy assessing and researching, and now they had got to writers and would I please come and be assessed? "Our way of conducting research is to invite selected subjects to come to the Institute house for a period of two or three days, and there talk with members of our staff, participate in a series of experiments and psychological tests, and meet and interact with a number of other persons selected on a familiar basis." Lady Ottoline Morrel used to do the same thing, but she had to use her own money, and to judge from Aldous Huxley's novel the interacting was more fun. Anyway—the novel made him famous. The IPAR *née* OS of OSS, didn't sound like quite such profitable literary material but it promised to be fun enough.

So I drove over to the remodeled fraternity house that

sheltered this American politisolator of dreadfully civilized vivisection, across the bridge in the sunset under the
dog and the cone and the still beeping balls, wondering if I
really was ever going to escape from the lot of this hilariously sarcastic Russian movie I have been lost in for the
past ten years. Everybody was so nice. I met people I knew,
looking sheepish, and Jungians looking like séance addicts
about to get a message from the Beyond, and clinical psychologists looking like Buick dealers, and psychiatrists
fresh from the loony wards looking tired and worried, and
professors looking like professors, and specialists in the
creative personality (believe me, it is possible to make a
living at this specialty) with the shy, happy, chummy look
of specialists in the creative personality, and a couple of
rugged sharpies who looked like they were in it for kicks,
and several earnest and not very happy young women.

Cocktails. How I hate them. This social obligation to
stick your tongue on a third rail before dinner—the only
universally accepted Rite of Passage of modern civilization. They had cocktails at Yalta, cocktails at the coming
out party of *The Memoirs of an Escaped Nun,* cocktails at
weddings, at births, at gallery openings, maybe at hang-
ings, and here we were being bucked up for our mental de-
lousing with the things again. I had a little whiskey. It
didn't make the dinner taste any worse. I began to realize
I was back in America, a place I try to keep away from.
The conversation was all about children and television. It
sounded awfully cooked and loaded, but I put that down
to everybody being self-conscious—"a little paranoid" as

67

they say. For what it was worth, they learned that I have never seen a complete TV program and my children don't watch it. We don't own a set or have any friends who do. I wasn't aggressive about it; in fact, it all came out slowly and politely and reluctantly. After dinner everybody paired off for Rorschachs. I have become down the years a little fatigued with Rorschachs and my normal powers of fantasy always desert me, but I strung along—you can't win. And then those terribly corny thematic pictures with which I have never been able to do anything whatever. And then some questionnaires, and I guess about then the Terman test, that tour de force of conformity. By this time everybody was weary and we called it a night.

The night, at their expense, was to be spent in the Hotel Claremont. This is a curious place. It is an immense, flamboyant wooden structure, built in Stanford White's own "California style" either by him or by a close disciple, and worthy of the wildest moments of Barcelona's wonderful lunatic. It is just across the bridge from San Francisco, that notoriously cosmopolitan city, but it is, weekends, the hangout of Berkeley's leading small merchants and their wives or stenographers—a more provincial lot than ever existed in Brooklyn's innermost recesses in its most recessive days. Like Toynbee and Berenson, I have long struggled to devise a definition and etiology of provincialism. As the late evening drug away I had plenty of chance to ponder it. I felt like Edmund Wilson that time his plane got forced down in Miami and he was forced down into twenty-four hours of the Great American Mass Culture about which he had written often and learnedly and in innocent and utter ignorance.

This was it. What country was I in? Where was my passport? Suddenly I ran onto the daughter of a leading libertarian intellectual, working like a dog as one of the institution's better dressed menialities. We were both plenty startled. What was I doing here? When she asked, I realized the answer. I was making a fast buck allowing my head to be tooken apart by skilled representatives of precisely this world, here tonight disporting itself in ill-fitting lamé creations and Sears Roebuck tuxedos. Tonight they might buy me drinks or even dance with me. But tomorrow, off in the tortuous *couloirs* of a remodeled fraternity house, the billions of Mr. Carnegie and the penetrating insights of Drs. Jung and Terman were going to concentrate on my poor central nervous system and find out why I couldn't mix in with a dinner dance in Fargo, North Dakota, and what it would mean to the OS of the OSS of the onrushing ICBM War III. Oh but I could. Only Mr. Luce thinks I'm like Rimbaud. I'm a great mixer . . . but I missed my wife and kids, so I went to bed.

All next day it went on. I made up a picture out of little bits of color. I had a long, chummy, deep-speaking-to-deep, sort of talk with the expert on the creative personality. I indicated my preferences in Scotch tartans. I chased the elusive gestalts through lines of bric-a-brac. I sought the still more elusive after-images of melodies like *Humoresque* and noises like something falling down. I sorted things and interpreted symbols. A rather frightened, puzzled, but very determined looking young woman took me in the attic, blindfolded me, led me into a dark room, and spent twenty minutes finding out if I could tell vertical from horizontal. Honest to God, cross my heart, hope to die. I could, pretty good.

Cocktails in the gloaming again and then some more of that exquisite *cuisine institutionale Americaine,* and then lots of questionnaires. One was by two Jungian ladies and was it something! It was probably the best autoanalysis of two Jungian ladies ever done. I wouldn't like to know them. They were mortifyingly shy in mixed company. They said the wrong things when out socially and then regretted them bitterly in the wee hours. They didn't like their complexions. They didn't like men. Not even Carl Jung. They were real foul-ups. You could tell from the questionnaire. Fortunately they didn't appear in the flesh, just their most distressing questionnaires. And then the long pink ones they give the kids at Cal. Very appropriate for middle-aged, successful authors. "Would you like to be a fireman?" "Do you ever doze off in class?" "Does your family object when you stay out late?"—as well as a number of subtly loaded questions which add up to, "Are you bothered much by the sin of impure touch?" By the time I got through I had a darn good notion to just up and bite my nails. The next day drug on with more of the same until afternoon when we got more cocktails and had a chummy little summing-up and were all very polite to each other. I think the term in these cats' jive is "shared each other's thinking." Oh, yeah?

What did it all mean? Nothing. The sensory tests meas-
ured responses and faculties in ways open to subjective
distortion both by the subject and the examiner. The very
mild psychoanalytic probings were utterly superficial and,
as far as I could judge, inspired entirely by the dubious
occultism of the Swiss mahatma. All psychoanalysts I have
ever known have struck me as being writers *manqué* to
a man and most of them either hate and fear the creative
artist, like Freud, or pay him the silly adulation of the
amateur sorceresses of the menopause circuit, the swami
and sonnet girls of the late Helen Hokinson—like Jung.
The serious ones are far too busy in clinics and hospitals
trying to help the really mentally ill to bother with nonsense like this. The vertical and horizontal girl was all
right. You felt she had something there and was grimly
resolved to find out if it meant anything. Seriously, though,
she was testing a measurable, physical response; it was a
poor thing, but science and her own. I would have felt
much better all around if my reflexes had been hammered
and they'd have found out if I was dermographic, if my
irises responded properly to stimuli, if my feet sweat, if I
swallowed air or was subject to fits of unmotivated itching.
"Does your family object if you stay out late?" "Do you
think your poems up, or do they just come to you?" Indeed!

Basic Books has just published a book in which a similar
bunch of clinical psychologists have tested three groups,
the normal (?), the neurotic (?), the psychotic (?), in a
similar way. What did they discover after spending a lot

71

of foundation money? That the normal were normal, the psychotics weren't, and the neurotics were nervous. Really they did, I'm telling the truth. In other words, this unvarnished hokum with which our society intimidates itself is far less effective—far less scientific—than the varnished hokum of other days and peoples. Any Sioux medicine man, any kind and attentive priest, any properly aged grandmother, any Chinese herbalist, could have found out more in a half hour than these people did in three days. And they, or people like them, could have any time in the past ten thousand years at least. I for one would, if I had my rathers, far rather trust myself to the boys in horns and bearskins who painted the Altamira cave.

It was all done so much more cheaply, too. That is the point. The whole point. These capers have been going on for years. The OS of the OSS and the IPAR are doing poets now only because they are scraping the bottom of their social barrel. They've already done just about every other category of human being. This has cost many large buckets of money. A foundation, no more than the government, is not a money bush. Once that money was somebody's labor. As the old socialist teachers used to say in the Rand School when I was a child, "Who are the eaters of surplus value?" All this foundation jive is just a very fancy way of exploiting the working class. It has replaced the "Radical Movement" as the great source of interesting careers for the unemployable children of the middle and upper classes . . . like India or the Church in nineteenth-century England. America is full of Phi Beta Kappas in well-shined shoes who toil not, neither do they spin. They have projects. And the profits of the oil wells in Arabia and the automobile factories in Detroit and the steel mills in Pittsburgh feed them and clothe them and shelter them like the lilies of the field and the foxes of the earth. They are just another way of circumventing the falling rate of profit and about as socially useful as an intercontinental ballistic missile. All this sort of nonsense—production for social waste—has taken the place of colonialism in mid-twentieth-century economy. A clinical psychologist living on a steelworker's unpaid wages is fulfilling exactly the same social function as one of Masefield's famous "cheap tin trays" outward bound down the greasy Channel to the reluctant Fuzzy Wuzzys. No more, no less.

As for clinical psychology itself, and/or psychoanalysis, does experience substantiate any of their vast claims? The sick and troubled in this sick and troubled society need help desperately, and wise and loving people can help them. If their medicine bundles full of rats' teeth and oddly shaped pebbles and bats' dung give them the necessary confidence to inspire reciprocal confidence in their patients, well and good. But when Ernest Jones says that if he could have got Hitler and Mussolini and Stalin and Churchill and Roosevelt on his couch he could have changed history, we are dealing with a badly self-deluded thaumaturgist. As for an operation like the OS of the OSS, now called IPAR, it is posited on the assumption of the relative benignity of the society that will make use of its findings, granting that it will turn up bona fide findings. Theoretically this happy-

73

go-lucky invasion of the sanctity of the person, this analysis
of the sources of creativity and non-conformity, could be
put to the most vicious uses. Not after some dictator has
seized power—but simply in the due course of our obviously accelerating decay of liberty and respect for the person. As I pointed out to a well-known Irish novelist who
was a fellow hamster, neither Thomas Paine nor Robert
Emmett would have submitted to such indignities for an
instant. We take them as a normal part of our society. This
is all true, but one assumption is false. There is no evidence that all this stuff works. It doesn't. There isn't the
slightest evidence that the puddler in Pittsburgh, the man
on the line in River Rouge, is one iota happier for all the
millions of his wages spent on industrial psychologists.
And as for the other side of the coin, Stalin presumably
had at his disposal the talents of some of the world's finest
clinical psychologists, trained in the most rigorous of
schools, and yet, according to Khrushchev, when it came to
a showdown in the cork-lined cellars, all the drugs and
brainwashing and psychology proved ineffective and the
confessions of the Moscow Trials were produced by techniques older far than those of medicine men or the Nean-
derthal witch doctors of the caves. Courage and common
sense are the first of virtues, as Johnson said. A brave man
can take a lot of punishment, a sensible man can see
through a lot of fraud. I don't really think we have much
to fear from a dictatorship serviced by psychologists, and
it is nice ours don't even believe in hurting you, even to the
extent of a back scratch or a tap on the knee, yet.

# SAMUEL BECKETT
# AND THE IMPORTANCE
# OF WAITING

Although Sam Beckett has been around for a good many years, Roger Blin's production of *Waiting for Godot—En Attendant Godot*—at the Théâtre Babylone, several years ago in Paris, seems to have, as the fellow said, catapulted him into an international reputation overnight. Tennessee Williams is reported of the opinion that *Godot* is the greatest play since Pirandello's *Six Characters in Search of an Author*. Right off let me say that I agree with him. Furthermore, I think *Molloy* is the most significant—laying aside the question of greatness—novel published in any language since World War II.

Beckett is so significant, or so great, because he has said the final word to date in the long indictment of industrial and commercial civilization which began with Blake, Sade, Hoelderlin, Baudelaire, and has continued to our day with Lawrence, Céline, Miller, and whose most forthright recent voices have been Artaud and Genet.

Now this is not only the mainstream of what the squares call Western European culture—by which they mean the culture of the capitalist era—it is really all the stream there is. Anything else, however gaudy in its day, has proved to be beneath the contempt of history. This is a singular phenomenon. There has been no other civilization in history whose culture-bearers never had a good word to say for it. Sam Beckett—an Irishman who has lived in France and written in French (his books are translated for publication in English) most of his adult life—raises the issue of what is wrong with us with particular violence because his indictment is not only the most thoroughgoing but also the sanest. It is easy enough to write off Lautréamont, who seems to have literally believed that the vulva of the universe was going to gobble him up, or Artaud, who believed that bad little people inhabited his bowels. The cyclone fence around the madhouse is certainly a great comfort. The trouble is that Sam Beckett is on this side of the fence. He is not only an artist of consummate skill who has learned every lesson from everybody who had anything to teach at all—from Lord Dunsany to Marcel Proust and Gertrude Stein (compare the actual plot of *Godot* with that old little theater chestnut of Dunsany's called something like *The Pearly Gate*)—he also has a mind of singular toughness and stability, a mind like an eighteenth-century Englishman, as sly as Gibbon, as compassionate as Johnson, as bold as Wilkes, as Olympian as Fielding. I don't mean that he is "as good as" a mixture of all these people. I mean he is their moral contemporary. "Courage, sir," said Johnson to Boswell.

Beckett refuses to run off to Africa and die of gangrene, or write childish poems to prostitutes, or even see angels in a tree. If you can drive your prophets mad, you don't have to bother to crucify them. When a prophet refuses to go crazy, he becomes quite a problem, crucifixion being as complicated as it is in humanitarian America. However, when *Godot* was put on in Miami, certain critics, no doubt instantly recognizing themselves as two of the leading characters in the play, turned on it with a savagery remarkable even for them. They're smart, these fellows, smarter than you think. Of course, part of this—the illiterate and vindictive reception of the play and of Beckett's novel by the majority of American critics, is just Gresham's Law operating after its accustomed wont—bad money driving out good. It is obvious that if there were twenty *Godot*-like plays on Broadway and a hundred *Molloy*-like novels on the counters of the bookshops, a lot of other plays and novels wouldn't be there.

One of the most remarkable things about the reception of Beckett in America is the large amount of favorable notice he has received—not just in the quarterlies and *The Nation, The New Republic,* and *Commonweal,* but in the small-town book columns scattered all over the country. I have just finished reading an envelope of clippings which Barney Rosset of Grove Press was kind enough to send me when I told him I was doing this article. I feel much better than I did after reading the critical welcome of *Godot* when it opened in Miami. Things are looking up. Voices are being raised. We may painfully crawl over the hump into semicivilization yet.*

---

* Since this was written, *Godot* has been put on as a "floor show" in the *Crystal Palace* in St. Louis, a civilized night club run by Jay and Fred Landesman, and has run for a whole season to packed houses in San Fran-

The European reception of Beckett in the last couple of years, as you know if you keep up with things over there, has been, to put it mildly, dizzying. He has become an international public figure like Lollobrigida or Khrushchev. Sam Beckett's first published work was a six-page pamphlet, *Whoroscope* (Nancy Cunard, the Hours Press, Paris, 1930). This is a poem, like the poems we were all writing then—at least I was, and Louis Zukovsky, and Walter Lowenfels, and a few other people—very disassociated and recombined, with two pages of notes. Its point is that although René Descartes kept his own birthdate to himself so that no astrologer could cast his nativity and believed that an omelet made of eggs more or less than eight days under the hen was disgusting, although he separated spirit and matter and considered man an angel riding a bicycle, mortality caught up with him and the spirit betrayed him— the angel wore out the bicycle and the bicycle abraded the angel. This has remained one of Beckett's main themes— what is mortality for? And the point of view has never changed. That is, he has carefully pared away from what they call his universe of discourse everything except those questions which cannot be answered. He gives plenty of

---

cisco. *Godot's* popular success, musicians like Charles Mingus, jazz-poetry concerts, and commentators like Mort Sahl have produced a revolution in the entertainment business—"the freak gig, San Francisco style" night club. This is enormously profitable—and *Variety* and *Billboard* have changed their tune. Former Bowery barrooms now give quartet recitals of Boulez and William Byrd, and there aren't enough *Godots* to meet the demand. Unfortunately this great popularity of very highbrow entertainment in small clubs and coffee rooms in the U.S.A. or on the B.B.C. has led to a distinct odor of formula—presage of real commercialization. Riesman is only too right.

answers: Pozzo and Lucky in *Godot*—the sempiternal master and man—are, of course, an answer. And, of course, an irrelevant answer. They owe their existence, as does all the "matter"—in Aristotle's sense—of Beckett's art, to their irrelevance.

In 1931, he did a little job of work for Chatto and Windus, a 72-page guide to Proust, a masterpiece of irascible insight worthy to rank with Jonson on Savage. It is one of the very best pieces of modern criticism and it is difficult to resist quoting it extensively. In fact, the best thing to do would be just to throw away everything I've written and substitute selected sentences from Beckett on Proust. In the concluding pages, he says, "The quality of language is more important than any system of ethics or aesthetics . . . form is the concretion of content, the revelation of a world. . . . He assimilates the human to the vegetal. . . . His men and women are victims of their volition—active with a grotesque, predetermined activity within the narrow limits of an impure world . . . but shameless. . . . The . . . stasis is contemplative, a pure act of understanding, will-less, the 'amabilis insania.' . . . From this point of view, opera is less complete than vaudeville, which at least inaugurates the comedy of an exhaustive enumeration. . . . In one passage, he describes the recurrent mystical experience as a purely musical impression, non-extensive, entirely original, irreducible to any order of impression— *sine materia* . . . the invisible reality that damns the life of the body on earth as a pensum and reveals the meaning of the word defunctus." The most cursory reading of five pages of *Molloy* or *Godot* will reveal the present significance of these words in the practice of Beckett himself.

*Murphy* (London, 1938; Paris, 1947; New York, 1957) went unnoticed in the blizzard of "social" literature. It is the story of the quest for the person in terms of the quest for a valid asceticism. At the end Murphy has not found himself because he has not found what he can validly do without or safely do with. He may be on the brink of such a discovery, but mortality overtakes him. It is as though Arjuna had been poleaxed in his chariot while Krishna rambled sententiously.

*Watt* was written in 1945 but published in Paris in 1953 and in New York in 1959. "Watt" is the Irish pronunciation of "What." It is a step forward in the best possible medium for Beckett's vision—the grim humor of *Iphigenia in Tauris, Lear,* Machiavelli's *Mandragola,* and Jonson's *Volpone.* Its concern is the problem: Who is who, and its corollary: What is what. To quote: "Looking at a pot, for example, or thinking of a pot, at one of Mr. Knott's pots, of one of Mr. Knott's pots, it was in vain that Watt said, Pot, pot. Well, perhaps not quite in vain, but very nearly. For it was not a pot, the more he looked, the more he reflected, the more he felt sure of that, that it was not a pot of which one could say, Pot, pot, and be comforted." If you don't understand, you can substitute Watt for Pot and vice versa. And I hope you notice the sentence, "Well, perhaps not quite in vain, but very nearly." Because that is the gist of the matter and the plot of the novel—the point, so to speak. And it is the point of a good deal of Beckett.

*Molloy*, published in New York and Paris in 1955, is the story of two journalists, two keepers of personal, disorganized journals in the dark, light years beyond the end of night. One, Molloy, a cripple, is left eventually on his belly in the gloom, clawing his way forward with his crutches. Possibly he is seeking his mother—at least at times that is the impression. Eventually he crawls to a room somewhere where "they"—the "they" of Edward Lear's limericks—bring him food and writing material and take away for their own purposes his narrative as he writes it week by week. It is a grim reverie of empty progress through time and space, punctuated with dog-like sex and paretic battle.

Moran, the subject of the second half of the novel, is a more recognizable literary figure—the hunter with all the characteristics of the hunted. Inspector Maigret with the personality of Gregor. The detective in *Crime and Punishment* replaced by Smerdyakov from *Karamazov*. At the orders of a hidden boss whom Beckett, with a minimum of effort (his name—Youdi—and his otherwise dense anonymity) invests with the terrors of Fu Manchu. At this impersonal force's behest, Moran hunts Molloy. In the process he loses his son and all the appurtenances of his personality, and becomes indistinguishable from his quarry. At the end he possibly encounters and kills Molloy without knowing it. On crutches himself, in the night, in the rain, he discovers a voice, and writes in turn his narrative.

*Molloy* is the drama, totally devoid of event, of relevant

81

event, of the seekers and the finders, of whom it has been said, "Finders keepers, losers weepers."

In *Malone Dies* (Paris, 1951; New York, 1955), Malone is another lonely writer, locked in a room and fed like a beast. He is trying to find his own existence by, as it were, describing his anti-self, by describing a hero who will be progressively differentiated from Malone, but he cannot do it. He cannot even keep track of the other's name, and he finally comes to write a story that sounds like an exhausted Sade, and which is, of course, the story of Malone.

*The Unnameable* (Paris, 1953; New York, 1958), is exactly what its title says—the narrative of someone without a name who cannot find a name, who never does.

*Waiting for Godot,* produced in New York in 1956, is that rare play, the distillation of dramatic essence which we have been talking about for the whole twentieth century, and about which we have done, alas, so little. Its peers are the Japanese Noh drama and the American burlesque comedy team. It is not just a play of situation—a situation which, in the Japanese Noh drama, reveals its own essence like a crystal. It just is a situation. The crystal isn't there. Two tramps, two utterly dispossessed, alienated, and disaffiliated beings, are waiting for somebody who is never going to come and who might be God. Not because they have any faith in his coming, although one does, a little, but because waiting requires less effort than anything else. They are not seeking meaning. The meaning is in the waiting. They are interrupted by the eruption into their contemplative lives of "The World"—"Western Civilization"

—or anything else like that which might be put in capital letters—in the persons of Pozzo and Lucky, Master and Man—two cacophonous marionettes of stunning horror. In their second appearance Pozzo and Lucky grow even more horrible and considerably less stunning. Otherwise, time does not pass. Today cannot recall yesterday, and tomorrow is not coming. The meaning is in the waiting. And in the tree, which overnight, between the acts, manages a few flimsy leaves. In the void, Beckett's tramps idle, analogues of Kanzan and Jitoku, the clown saints of Zen. Vladimir says, "Well, shall we go?" Estragon says, "Yes, let's go." Beckett says, *They do not move. Curtain.*"

Theatrically speaking, in terms of an evening's entertainment, I have given a falsely bleak picture. The play is actually hilariously funny. All the traditional business that has come down from the Romans through Italian comedy to burlesque, to the red-nosed, derby-hatted, baggy-pantsed burlesque clown, is exploited. But it is not exploited in its own terms. Each passage of business worthy of Chaplin or Buster Keaton at his best, is transmuted with a terrible light—the fire of some final judgment—like the deadly ray of unimaginable colors from some other spectrum that shines in science fiction.

I think this summary of his achievement to date and its meaning has been fair to Beckett. Now there is nothing left, since I have already implied that he is an artist of consummate attainment, but an attempt to answer the question, since he is a moral artist, is it true? Do these books represent a valid judgment of the human situation? I do not want to sound like an editorial in *Pravda,* but I doubt it, partly. It is not absolutely true at its most superficial level. The world ill, *le mal mondial,* is not only limited in time to the last two hundred years, but it is limited in space to that very little peninsula, Europe, and to the new lands Europe has overrun. I realize that it is imbecilic to say, "Why doesn't Sam Beckett (or Artaud or Céline or Miller) sing the glories of our Stakhanovite workers and collectivist farmers and tractor drivers, or of our jet pilots and cobalt atom splitters? Where is the New Man, the Hero of the Twentieth Century?" And all critics who object to Beckett reduce themselves eventually to this level, the level of Zhadnov, *Variety,* and the quarterly reappearing lead editorial in *Time's* book section. Nonetheless, the light is never spent. Heroism is only smoldering and will flame up after these dark ages are over. The society in which we live is destroying the person and the communion of persons. First we must define and find the person, the self and the other—you and me—(not Kierkegaard's Godot—the "utterly other")—that is the current problem, the superficial "message" of Beckett's books, and it is, historically, superficial and temporary.

As for the permanent one, not superficially: this is Beckett's main subject, and here his judgment is not invalid, because it is the judgment of Homer, of the literature of heroes. The world is blind, and random. If we persist in judging it in human terms it is malignant and frivolous. Only man is loyal and kind and brave. Only man loves. Aphrodite ruts like her pigeons. Zeus thunders like the empty sky. If we refuse to accept the world on secular terms, Godot isn't coming. If we accept it for ourselves, the comradeship of men, whether verminous tramps with unmanageable pants or Jim and Huck Finn drifting through all the universe on their raft—the comradeship of men in work, in art, or simply in waiting, in the utterly unacquisitive act of waiting, is an ultimate value—so ultimate that it gives life sufficient dignity and satisfaction. So say Homer and Sam Beckett and anybody else, too, who has ever been worth his salt.

# WOULD YOU HIT A WOMAN
# WITH A CHILD, OR WHO
# WAS THAT LADY I SEEN YOU
# WITH LAST NIGHT?

"What, sir," said Boswell, notebook in hand, "is the principal virtue?" "Whereas, sir," said Sam, "you know, courage is reckoned the greatest of all virtues; because unless a man has that virtue, he has no security for preserving any other."

When Bob Hatch wrote and suggested we have a piece on the decline of American humor for the *Nation*'s Spring Book Issue [1957], I said fine, we can use Columbia's new collection of Vance Randolph and somebody else's selection of Finley Peter Dunne as pegs to hang it on; few things are funnier and fewer things today are anything like them. Unfortunately, the books never came, so this story will have to be more general and sort of anticipatory.

I don't know about the new selection of Mr. Dooley. Just recently I read some professor who said he was an Irish dialect comedian, so, since this editor is probably a professor too, it may be a pig in a poke. But there is no doubt about Vance Randolph. He has never published a book that wasn't thoroughly satisfying, and he has done some five or six I know of: *Who Blowed Up the Church House?*, *The*

*Devil's Pretty Daughter, We Always Lie to Strangers, Ozark Superstitions,* all with Columbia, and *Down in the Holler* (with George P. Wilson), with the University of Oklahoma Press. Get them all, and the new one, too. This isn't TV hillbilly humor, it isn't even Al Capp or Erskine Caldwell. It is a last lingering contact with an older and better world, a thin red umbilicus still attached to what Sherwood Anderson would have called the American Earth. I am well aware that the reason for the popularity of the cultural survivals of the Southern Highlands on the New York stage is that barefoot girls and one-gallus, corn-cob-bearing males give the subway Neanderthals somebody to look down on—no mean accomplishment. The real thing is something else again. Vance Randolph is *not* a professor, but an uncorrupted amateur folklorist. This is a great tradition, all the best folklore we have has been collected by doctors (of medicine, not philosophy), clergymen, school-marms, and plain people. There is something about the methodology of scholarship that blights folkspeech.

Everybody knows that the Southern Highlands are the last refuge of the American frontier, and, from before our own, of the marches of England and Scotland and of the Scots and North Irish. But there is more to the Ozarks than Toynbee's "external proletariat." This is the home of the Green Corn Rebellion, the land where, in the evenings, around the stove in the crossroads store, one literate farmer read aloud the words of Oscar Ameringer and *The Appeal to Reason,* slowly and painfully, to the leg-slapping approval of a tobacco-chewing audience. Here, if anywhere

87

in America, was the focus of a purely indigenous agrarian anarchist-socialism. I have run hounds, swapped lies, and drunk tiger piss with men who would have been happy fighting with Makhno. Unruly, utterly skeptical, absolutely fearless, bawdy free-thinkers—very different indeed from the originals of the term "square"—the square-headed agrarian Progressives of the northern Middlewest. These are the key words of great—classic—epic—Homeric— humor. A sense of the consistent principle of incongruity on which Nature, for all our science and philosophy, really operates. The realization that the accepted, official version of anything is most likely false and that all authority is based on fraud. The courage to face and act on these two conclusions. The appreciation of the wonderful hilarity of the processes of human procreation and elimination. The acceptance of the prime fact that nobody made it that way —it just happened. I find it hard to bust into roars of laughter over the long-winded racket of the majority of the old-time humorists Constance Rourke writes about. I am not a passionate devotee of Sut Lovingood. But from those days to Mencken—or even Westbrook Pegler, Damon Runyon, or Will Rogers at their best, these were the qualities that made American humor American. It was just plain lack of style that made it, in so many cases, tedious.

This, once, was the blood and meat and bone of our very own life. Out of it came our one epic hero, the only American who can walk with Ajax and Odysseus—Huck Finn. What happened to this heritage? I'll tell you what happened to it. Not long ago, in the *Vaticide Review,* a college professor who, of all things, teaches the children of cowboys in a university in the mountains of the Wild West, wrote a "paper" conclusively demonstrating by patient, laborious research that *Huckleberry Finn* was a homosexual romance. This came about, not because the professor was himself a homosexual, but because he was moribund with the ultimate corruption of human self-alienation. He just didn't know what the word "work" meant. He had never done any. He never knew anybody who had done any. *Huckleberry Finn* is our example of one of the three or four basic epic plots—maybe there are really only two. It is about the devoted comradeship of men at grips with a "morally neuter"—frivolous, the Greeks called their gods —environment, the inchoate and irresponsible flux of the universe, on which men, *working* in comradeship, impose the order of their virtues and their reason. And the first of these is courage.

Life is all a great joke—but only the brave ever get the point. When James, W. not H., said, "It is true if it works," this very frontier, American sort of thing, is what he meant. He meant, "If you can do *work* with it." Only truth can impose order on the environment of disorder. Our professor at a cowtown university undoubtedly thinks it means "if you can 'work' some kind of finagle with it." The reason pragmatism got such a bad name is that it came to be taught by people who did not *work* their way through school at jobs, but as teaching assistants. Incongruity? Yes—but laughter comes with the mastery of incongruity, like handling logs in a spring river, tossing sacks of wheat into a box car, making babies, or cutting a cam that works just right on your own machine. When August Kekule saw his benzine ring, he laughed. In the *Lankavatara Sutra,* Buddha laughed at the vision of compound infinitudes of universes. The great Turner picture is of "Ulysses *Deriding* Polyphemus." The tiny figure on its gaily caparisoned boat is *laughing* at the bellowing man mountain. The *Odyssey* is a comedy.

Once these qualities go from humor it becomes sicklied o'er with the pale cast of effeminacy. Compare Dorothy Parker or Ogden Nash with Lear: "There was an old man who said, 'Hush,/I think there's a bird in this bush.'/When they said, 'Is it small?'/he replied, 'Not at all./It's three times the size of the bush.' " Whimsey, like black lace underwear, is all right in its place. Great humor has a savagery about it. This is why British humor stands up better than American in this century—particularly British bawdry. All the great dirty limericks, like detective stories, have English settings. It's like English cooking, which is still that of Boadicea's day. True conservatives, the English have yet to wash off all their woad. It is for this reason that, however subversive of the established order, so many great humorists, especially satirists, Roman or British, have been Tories. The revolutionary action of humor is a deeper thing than any current politics, and the humorist tends to adopt these social attitudes which at least claim to insure him the strongest connections with the oldest, most fundamental, most human behavior.

In America, by and large, this has not been true. You

90

can, or at least T. S. Eliot can, create a "myth of conserva-
tism," but it is pretty damn hard to work up any myth of
the American business community. Henry Luce has spent
billions trying and is still working at it, but all the progress
reports are negative. We do not usually think of Damon
Runyon as a radical, but go back and read the workingstiff
dialect poetry he wrote when the century was young. "It
pays to git a plenty while you're gittin'." And I will never
forget the time I heard Will Rogers say, "I hear the Standard Oil Company has adopted the motto, 'We Serve the
Public.' Havin' growed up on a farm, I know jist what
they're a' gittin' at." We forgive Mencken his beer-cellar
Nietzscheism. We forget that years ago, Pegler was hired
by Scripps-Howard for the same reason Heywood Broun
was—he was a "fearless independent," not a gutta-percha
bottle of corrosive rancors. By and large, though, American
humor until well into this century has been "radical." All
humor *must be* in the etymological sense. Ours was also
in the political. Out of the *Masses,* old and *New,* came the
major cartoonists of the period. Still unsurpassed, many
of them are famous today. The whole lithograph crayon
technique, so closely identified with Buck Ellis and Bob
Minor, and originally developed for the I.W.W. press, has
about it the very essence of completely autonomous, completely autochthonous, American workingstiff defiance.

Finley Peter Dunne (Mr. Dooley) is the author of:
"Wan iv th' strangest things about life is that th' poor, who
need th' money th' most, ar-re th' very wans that niver
have it." "Don't ask f'r rights. Take thim. An' don't let

91

anny wan give thim to ye. A right that is handed to ye fer nawthin' has somethin' the mather with it. It's more thin likely it's ony a wrrong turned inside out." " 'Tis a sthrange thing whin we come to think iv it that th' less money a man gits f'r his wurruk, th' more nicissary it 'tis to th' wurruld that he shud go on wurrukin'. Yer boss kin go to Paris on a combination weddin' and divorce thrip an' no one bothers his head abouth him. But if ye shud go to Paris—excuse me laughin' mesilf black in th' face—th' industhrees iv th' country pine away." "Mebbe 'tis as bad to take champagne out of wan man's mouth as it 'tis to take rround shteak out of anather's." "It takes vice t' hunt vice. That accounts f'r polismen." "I care not who makes th' laws iv a nation, if I can get out an injunction." "Laws are made t' throuble people, and th' more throuble they make th' longer they shtay on the shtachoo books." "If me ancestors were not what Hogan calls regicides, 'twas not because they wan't ready an' willin', ony a king niver came their way." "A constitootional ixicative, Hinissey, is a ruler who does as he damn pleases an' blames th' people."

What happened? Where did this kind of humor go? Don't forget, Dunne wrote this stuff for what they call the capitalist press. It went the same place the manual spark lever and the choke went on cars. They were dangerous because women used them to hang their purses on. Think of the environment in which Mr. Dooley was appreciated. Who rushes the growler today? How many people chew Piper Heidsieck? How many smoke Five Brothers in a corncob pipe? Humor must be about the basic verities.

The distinguishing mark of our contemporary humor, what has come to be called "*New Yorker* humor," is that it is of, for, and by the great bulk of our population who live in interminably busy idleness, who are never at grips with their environment, but who live by delegated powers and vicarious atonements. They are surrounded by the gadgets that appear in the advertising columns alongside; when they have to do something as elemental as driving a nail or mowing a lawn some whimsical disaster always takes place. Like the movies, nothing ever happens that would offend any conceivable group or section of the population, or in any way interfere with the sale of any commodity whatsoever. Nothing important must happen—it would be bad for business.

A few comic strips linger on, *Moon Mullins*, *The Katzenjammer Kids*, Williams' *Out Our Way*. I wonder what the TV generation thinks of them? A few towns still permit emasculated burlesque shows, but the comics are not allowed to distract from the interminable parade of strippers. Chaplin is self-exiled. American radicalism lost its sense of humor long ago. And of course "the media" chew up everything, songs, jokes, "personalities"—365 days times 24 hours—this is a forest fire which consumes all in its path. What is wrong with American humor is what is wrong with American life. It is commercialism. True humor is the most effective mode of courage.

# KENNETH PATCHEN, NATURALIST OF THE PUBLIC NIGHTMARE

Kenneth Patchen has recently published two books, *Hurrah for Anything* * and *When We Were Here Together*.† They are two big strides forward in his development as a poet. For my taste, there have always been two fields in which his stuff never quite came off: first, a peculiar topsy-turvy bitter whimsey; second, the sentimental love lyric. The little poems, each illustrated with one of Patchen's uniquely comic drawings, in *Hurrah for Anything* are free verse limericks. Patchen has gone back to the world of Edward Lear and interpreted it in terms of the modern sensibility of the disengaged, the modern comic horrors of *le monde concentrationaire*. It is as if, not a slick *New Yorker* correspondent, but the Owl and the Pussycat were writing up Hiroshima. In *When We Were Here Together*, the giggly coyness that defaced so much of Patchen's love poetry has vanished. These are grave, serious, immeasurably touching poems. They compare very favorably with the love poems of Paul Eluard or Rafael Alberti. In other words, they are amongst the very few poems of their kind, written by an American, which can compete confidently in

---

* Jonathan Williams, Highlands, N.C., 1957.
† New Directions, N.Y.C., 1958.

the international arena of contemporary "comparative literature."

Patchen is the only widely published poet of my generation in the United States who has not abandoned the international idiom of twentieth-century verse. He is the only one we have, to take these two books as examples, to compare with Henri Michaux or Paul Eluard. Twenty-five years ago no one would have prophesied such a comeuppance for what we then thought, and I still think, was the only significant tendency in American literature. What happened to the Revolution of the Word? Why is Patchen still there? Why did everybody else "sell out" or sink, like Louis Zukofsky, Parker Tyler, Walter Lowenfels, into undeserved obscurity? Why did American poetry, a part of world literature in 1920, become a pale, provincial imitation of British verse in 1957? We are back, two generations behind Australia.

Man thrives where angels die of ecstasy and pigs die of disgust. The contemporary situation is like a long-standing, fatal disease. It is impossible to recall what life was like without it. We seem always to have had cancer of the heart.

The first twenty-five years of the century were the years of revolutionary hope. Immediately after the First War, this hope became almost universal among educated people. There was a time when most men expected that soon, very soon, life was going to change; a new, splendid creature was going to emerge from its ancient chrysalis of ignorance, brutality, and exploitation. Everything was going to be different. Even the commonest, most accepted routines

95

of life would be glorified. Education, art, sex, science, invention, everything from clothing to chess would be liberated. All the soilure and distortion of ages of slavery would fall away. Every detail of life would be harmoniously, functionally related in a whole which would be the realization of those absolutes of the philosophers, the Beloved Community wedded to the Idea of Beauty.

We who were born in the early years of the century accepted that hope implicitly. It was impossible that any feeble hands could halt the whole tendency of the universe. This was not the Idea of Progress, of indefinite human perfectibility, now the whipping boy of reactionary publicists and theologians. The nineteenth century had believed that the world was going to go on becoming more and more middle class until the suburbs of London stretched from Pole to Pole. We believed that man's constant potential for a decent, simple, graceful life was bound to realize itself within a very few years, that the forces of wealth, barbarism, and superstition were too weak to resist much longer.

On August 29, 1927, Sacco and Vanzetti were executed with the connivance of the leading descendants of the New England libertarians. A cheap politician and a judge with the mind of a debauched turnkey were able to carry through this public murder in the face of a world of protest of unbelievable intensity, mass, and duration. When the sirens of all the factories in the iron ring around Paris howled in the early dawn, and the myriad torches of the demonstrators were hurled through the midnight air in Buenos Aires, the generation of revolutionary hope was over. The conscience of mankind went to school to learn methods of compromising itself. The Moscow trials, the Kuo Min Tang street executions, the betrayal of Spain, the Hitler-Stalin Pact, the extermination of whole nations, Hiroshima, Algiers—no protest has stopped the monster jaws from closing. As the years go on, fewer and fewer protests are heard. The spokesmen, the intellects of the world, have blackmailed themselves and are silent. The common man dreams of security. Every day life grows more insecure, and, outside America, more nasty, brutish, and short. The lights that went out over Europe were never relit. Now the darkness is absolute. In the blackness, well-fed, cultured, carefully shaven gentlemen sit before microphones at mahogany tables and push the planet inch by inch towards extinction. We have come to the generation of revolutionary hopelessness. Men throw themselves under the wheels of the monsters, Russia and America, out of despair, for identical reasons.

With almost no exceptions, the silentiaries of American literature pretend that such a state of affairs does not exist. In fact, most of them do not need to pretend. They have ceased to be able to tell good from evil. One of the few exceptions is Kenneth Patchen. His voice is the voice of a conscience which is forgotten. He speaks from the moral viewpoint of the new century, the century of assured hope, before the dawn of the world-in-concentration-camp. But he speaks of the world as it is. Imagine if suddenly the men of 1900—H. G. Wells, Bernard Shaw, Peter Kropotkin, Romain Rolland, Martin Nexo, Maxim Gorky, Jack London—had been caught up, unprepared and uncompromised, fifty years into the terrible future. Patchen speaks as they would have spoken, in terms of unqualified horror and rejection. He speaks as Émile Zola spoke once—"A moment in the conscience of mankind." Critics have said of him, "After all, you can't be Jeremiah all the time." Indeed? Why not? As far as we know, all Jeremiah ever wrote was *The Book of Jeremiah* and the world of his day was a Chautauqua picnic in comparison with this.

It is not true, historically, that the poet is the unacknowledged legislator of mankind. On the contrary, poets seem to flourish under despotism. It is difficult to say if the artist and the prophet ever really merge. It is hard to find a common ground for Isaiah and Richard Lovelace. Artist and prophet seem perpetually at war in Blake and D. H. Lawrence. But there comes a point when the minimum integrity necessary to the bare functioning of the artist is destroyed by social evil unless he arise and denounce it. There is a subtle difference between the paintings of Boucher and the cover girls of American magazines. It is almost an abstract difference, like the difference between the North and South Poles—all the difference in the world. If the conscience remains awake, there comes a time when the practice of literature is intolerable dishonesty, the artist is overridden by the human being and is drafted into the role of Jeremiah.

Men in prison become obsessive. The prison itself is an objective obsession. Trotsky was paranoid, he saw assassins behind every bush. They were real assassins, as it turned out. On the other hand, men in madhouses console themselves by pretending they are kings in palaces. Patchen, very likely, is obsessed. Popinjay, on the other hand, refines his sensibilities with the accents of Donne and Hopkins. Writing this, sitting at my typewriter, looking out the window, I find it hard to comprehend why every human being doesn't run screaming into the streets of all the cities of the world this instant. How can they let it go on? Patchen doesn't. If no one cried, "Woe, woe to the bloody city of damnation!" and nobody listened to the few who cry out, we would know that the human race had finally gone hopelessly and forever mad.

There is no place for a poet in American society. No place at all for any kind of poet at all. Only two poets in my lifetime have ever made a living from their poetry—Edna Millay and Robert Frost. Neither of them would have done so if they had started their careers in the last two decades. The majority of American poets have acquiesced in the judgment of the predatory society. They do not exist as far as it is concerned. They make their living in a land of make-believe, as servants of a hoax for children. They are employees of the fog factories—the universities. They help make the fog. Behind their screen the universities fulfill their social purposes. They turn out bureaucrats, perpetuate the juridical lie, embroider the costumes of the delusion of participation, and of late, in departments never penetrated by the humanities staff, turn out atom, hydrogen, and cobalt bombers—genocidists is the word. Patchen fills these academicians with panic. "Let us walk, not run," says one of the best intentioned of them, "to the nearest exit. The bobbysoxers can have him." Let me out of here. Somebody is doing something frightfully embarrassing to all concerned. Precisely.

The bobbysoxers do have him. Against a conspiracy of silence of the whole of literary America, Patchen has become the laureate of the doomed youth of the Third World War. He is the most widely read younger poet in the country. Those who ignore him, try to pass over him, hush up his scandalous writings, are read hardly at all, unwillingly by their English students and querulously by one another. Years ago Patchen marked out his role. "I speak for a generation born in one war and doomed to die in another." Some of his most ambitious books were published by an obscure printer. Reviews of his work are almost all unfavorable. He is never published in the highbrow quarterlies. In a market where publishers spend millions to promote the masturbation fantasies of feeble-minded mammals, his books have made their way into the hands of youth, the hands that are being drafted to pull the triggers, the youth that is being driven to do the dying—for the feeble-minded mammals and their pimping publishers.

The official spokesmen of the Official Revolution have not chosen to stand in the place Patchen stands. Read Upton Sinclair's anthology, *The Cry for Justice* and any anthology of pseudo-proletarian literature of the Thirties. The contrast is shocking. From Patrick Magill to the young Sandburg and Lindsay, Oppenheim and Lola Ridge, the poets of the earlier day had an integrity, a moral earnest-

100

ness, which overrode their occasional corniness and gave them a substance of things hoped for, an evidence of things not seen, which has vanished from the work of the approved poets of bureaucratic salvation. "Change the world" indeed, but from what to what?

It has been pointed out, time out of mind, that American literature has never been whole. It has always split into two antagonistic tendencies: the exhortative, expressive, responsible, sometimes prophetic utterance—Whitman; and the egocentric, constructive, irresponsible *machine*—Poe. Today, in the epigoni of Henry James and the Corn College Donnes, the constructive tendency has degenerated to a point where it is no longer only irresponsible, but socially invisible. For better or worse, Patchen belongs to the first tendency. He shares the faults of Whitman, Sandburg at his early best, and e. e. cummings. His contemporary literary antagonists are practically faultless.

In a nation where every second English Department assistant is a provincial litterateur, a past master of the seven types of ambiguity to be found in Barnaby Googe, Patchen is one of the few representatives (Miller is another) of a world movement—Anti-Literature. He is a descendant of Sade, Restif, Lautréamont, Rimbaud, Corbière, Jarry, Apollinaire, a contemporary of Artaud. It is significant that in his case this ideology of creation has become quite conscious, even "class conscious" in a special sense.

*The Journal of Albion Moonlight* can be compared very aptly with Apollinaire's *Poet Assassinated*. There is an important difference. The assassins of Croniamantal, the poet, are Boredom and Misery, and the vagueness of the figure of the enemy gives Apollinaire's work an air of naïve imprecision which borders on frivolity. In Wyndham Lewis's *Childermass*, a similar book, the enemy is more carefully defined, but Lewis's impact is vitiated by the crankiness of his indictment. This is still more obvious if you compare Lewis's *The Apes of God* with Patchen's *Memoirs of a Shy Pornographer*. The *Apes* is certainly a great book, one of the monumental satires of our day, and it deals with events and issues of great importance. It also goes out of its way to pay off specific grudges against various denizens of Bloomsbury, Chelsea, and Charlotte Street. It ends with an extremely specific attack on the Sitwells. It is all very entertaining, but it is rather too monumental and you miss much of the fun if you don't know the people. The *Shy Pornographer* is not a *comédie à clef*. True, remarks like, "Have you anything in view?" need a footnote already, but there aren't too many of them.

On the whole, all three of Patchen's prose works deal with the "great archetypes," the same figures who are found in Homer, *Gulliver*, Rabelais, or *Le Morte D'Arthur*. But these dramatis personae have undergone a change unlike anything they ever experienced before. The actors, the masks, who have always spoken, in all the classics, the words of humanist culture, in epic, satire, comedy, or tragedy, have been reduced to their simplest elements and then filtered through the screen of the commodity culture. Launcelot becomes the Thin Man, Ulysses is worked over by Mickey Spillane, the Poet is confused with Flash Gordon, love scenes slip in and out of the idiom of *Ranch Romances*, Tristan and Iseult are played by Elvis Presley and Kim Novak. The idiom of science fiction or the blood-on-the-scanties school of detective stories accurately but naïvely reflects the mass psychosis, however skillfully it may be rigged to augment that psychosis and sell commodities. Patchen turns it upon itself, dissociates its elements, and uses them to create a vast, controlled, social dream, a diagnostic symbol of the collapse of civilization.

Patchen's active interference, so different from the passive madness of Lautréamont, is continuous in the texture of the narrative. His sentences are saturated with the acid of undeluded judgment, a running clinical commentary on the periods of Henry James, the oratory of the United Nations, the velleities of the literary quarterlies. Beside the narrative—the picture of the universal disorder of values and death of the sensibility—there runs this obbligato, the attack on literature, not out of any superficial épateism, but because the practice of literature today is the practice of acquiescence. This is a fundamental technique of all great comic writers; it is obvious in Erasmus, the *Letters of Obscure Men*, and Rabelais; but since that day humor has become a grimmer business. Characteristically, editors and critics cannot even comprehend the comic today, in this conspiracy of mutual guilt, mutual espionage, mutual silence. Imagine Gargantua, or Swift's savage indignation, or Nashe, or Lawrence's *Pansies*, or even *Absalom and Achitophel* in the pages of that refined quarterly which is devoted to perpetuating on a high-toned level the tradition of *Red Rock* and *The Birth of a Nation.*

The sort of thing Patchen does was written in France in the very brief period between the naïve revolt of Dada and the dissipation of all revolt in the deserts of Stalinist conformity or the swamps of neo-surrealist salon Freudianism. An example which occurs to me offhand is the early work of Aragon—which he, characteristically, no longer allows mentioned by his bibliographers. Was it he or Soupault who wrote a book of mockery called *The New Adventures of Nick Carter?* I no longer remember, but I do remember that it lacked Patchen's seriousness, his understanding of the real causes of the contemporary Black Death, his organized system of values, his solid vantage point of judgment. When Aragon deserted this medium, he said, "The newspapers present us daily with infinitely more horrible nightmares than we can manufacture in our studios." Patchen is well aware of this. *Albion Moonlight* and *Sleepers Awake,* not *Les Cloches de Basle,* are realistic portrayals of the modern world. Similarly, Patchen must be distinguished from the later, orthodox Surrealists. This stuff was largely a dreamy rehash of the troubles of rich women and their favorites of the literary, artistic, and pathic international. Rare, unhappy schoolboys here and there around the world may have read Breton once with excitement, but it takes modistes, comtesses, and American heiresses to read him with understanding. The nightmares of Patchen's narratives are the daily visions of millions.

Anti-literature is, of course, largely the real literature of certain epochs. Dynamite is one of the most powerful instruments of construction. One would think that any critic with a high school education would recognize the genre of *Don Quixote*. It is amazing to read the few reviews of Patchen's books that have ever been printed in the fashionable quarterlies. These little academic bunnies cannot even guess what he is about. Haven't they ever read *Don Quixote*, or *Tristam Shandy*, or *Gulliver*? The answer is no. They read one another in the fashionable quarterlies.

The other day one of the subalterns of the Bronx edition of *PMLA*, otherwise known as the *Vaticide Review*, said to me, "Patchen is no good, he has no feeling for the weight of words and no sense of literary responsibility." When I told him I was doing this piece he warned me, "Don't get tied up with Patchen. He'll destroy your reputation, just when you are getting recognition in the right circles." Un hunh. I have been around since the Twenties and have always had the recognition of my—or Patchen's—"right circles." I'll take a chance. To paraphrase old Steffie, I have seen the future and in some cases it wears bobby sox, at least for now.

# THE HASIDISM OF
# MARTIN BUBER

The last two years in the religious book field, it's been like
Old MacDonald's farm, with here a Buber, there a Buber,
everywhere a Buber, Buber. There is a good reason for this.
Martin Buber is practically the only religious writer a non-
religious person could take seriously today. Paul Tillich
probably runs him a close second, but Tillich is too much
a technical theologian for secular, let alone atheist, taste.
Yet Buber is one of the most important living theologians.
I should say that the determinative theological works of
this century have been Schweitzer's *Quest of the Historical
Jesus*, Otto's *The Idea of the Holy,* Barth's *Commentary on
the Epistle to the Romans,* and, to go back to the very beginning of the century, a selection, difficult to make, from
the works of Baron von Hugel and Father Tyrrell, and,
conversely, from the work of their opponents, the Neo-
Thomists, before Neo-Thomism became a fad with French
journalists and spoiled Surrealists. Towards the top of this
list belongs Buber's *I and Thou,* one of the most moving
books ever written.

*I and Thou* is a little book, a true pocket book, a *vade
mecum,* to go with you on your way, like *The Little Flowers
of St. Francis,* or Angelus Silesius, or *The Imitation of
Christ,* or the *Bhagavad-Gita,* or Carus' *Gospel of Buddha*
—"*vade mecum . . .*" and I imagine it has gone with

106

many a person on many a strange and tortured way. After
all, it is a book by a German Jew. I read it, long ago, in
French on the recommendation of—of all people—Hugh
MacDiarmid, and it was one of the determinative books of
my life. For twenty years I have given away copies of the
paperbound Scottish edition to whomever I could get interested. Scribner's announces a new edition of *I and Thou* for
this fall [1958]. That will mean that somewhere close to
twenty-five books by Martin Buber will be in print in English, many of them in paperback editions. A large number
of these latter have been published in the last two years.

What kind of religious writer is Martin Buber? He is a
Romantic Traditionalist. His approach to doctrine and
ritual is pragmatic, symbolist, experiential. This is a tradition, actually a kind of revolution, known to most educated
people as exemplified by Cardinal Newman, Father Tyrrell, Monsignor Duschene, Baron von Hugel, William
James, Carl Jung. Hard as it might be for the uninitiated
to believe, this was once the prevailing philosophy of the
Romanist clergy in America, until it was suppressed early
in the century by the famous Papal Bull against "Modernism." The great popularity of Carl Jung has led to its proliferation in every sect. In so far as they have any, it is the
philosophy of most occultists, Vedantists, self-styled Zen
Buddhists, a considerable percentage of Anglo-Catholics,
and a small but significant percentage of Roman Catholics
who, perforce, are not very communicative about it. Since
the terrible events of the war years it has become a common
attitude amongst previously non-religious Jews. It is not so

107

common amongst Protestants, for the reason that Protestantism does not provide this kind of an apologetic with sufficient materials to work on. These materials are myth, miracle, mystery, ritual, dogma. As far as the religious American Protestant layman is concerned, his religion has just spent three difficult centuries getting rid of precisely these characteristics and he does not care to return to them. Kierkegaard and Barth he never heard of; Reinhold Neibuhr he thinks of as a rather moralistic politician—like John Foster Dulles—and hence unreliable and unrealistic.

It is a clever apologetic, with a wonderful ability to sneak up on the most sophisticated and catch them unawares. Mystery, miracle, myth, ritual are considered anthropologically, in terms of their significance for a community—its living contact with its past, its internal coherence and tone, its ability to act in the present and envisage the future—exactly, of course, the way one would consider the role of religion in the study of an exotic primitive tribe. It is assumed that since some primitive tribes have been reported to be in a better state of social health than our admittedly sick civilization, the pervasive role of mystery, miracle, myth, ritual, is responsible for this difference. They give life dignity and significance, and with their rites of passage at birth, death, sexual maturity, marriage, eating, drinking, bathing—the matter of all sacraments everywhere—give it a kind of grandeur which lifts it out of the frustrations and tedium and ultimate meaninglessness of "materialistic existence." It is then assumed that since this constitutes social health, the individual in modern society who belongs to an artificial community which preserves these characteristics will have greater mental health than his non-religious fellows.

If miracle, mystery, myth, ritual, are group symbols of psychological realities which can be taken over by the individual to the great improvement of his mental health, why not dogma too? It is easier to believe an obvious impossibility—such as the Catholic doctrine that Christ came out of the Virgin's womb like light through glass and left her a *virgina intacta*, "Blessed Mary *Ever* Virgin,"—than it is to believe a simple misstatement of fact, for the simple reason that an impossibility, to be believed, must be immediately etherealized, made part of a system which is transmundane altogether. This is why so estimable a religion as Mormonism has so hard a time holding its young intellectuals. It is almost impossible to etherealize the simply wrong geography and history of the *Book of Mormon*. Anybody, even mathematical physicists, can believe the Athanasian Creed by an act of transfiguration of its statements.

So today we have large sections of our most literate population voluntarily adopting the religious behavior and beliefs of more primitive communities for purely pragmatic, psychologistic, personal reasons. The assumption is that this is a kind of symbolic behavior by which greater spiritual insight into reality, better interpersonal relations, and finally true realization of the self, will follow. The fact that there is not the slightest statistical evidence for this

109

assumption does not matter. The fact that the entire Judaeo-Christian-Muslim period in human history has been an episode of unparalleled personal and social psychosis and international barbarity is beside the point. People have Hanukkah lights in the window or Christmas trees at the winter solstice and take Communion at Easter or make a Seder on Pesach because the society in which they live provides them with no valid life aim and robs them of all conviction of personal integrity. All "neo" religions are cults of desperation in a time of human self-alienation and social disintegration. Rigid orthodoxies like Neo-Thomism are just archaizing pragmatisms of the same kind which as a final act of faith reject the personal and social instrumentalism which is their initial assumption.

It is in this context—that of the only effective apologetic of our time—that Buber functions. But this is not to belittle him. It is obvious that what I have been describing is not really the role of religion in society at all. It is the role of art. Just as the Surrealists and others have tried to substitute art for religion, so the Romantic Traditionalist, be he Jew, Catholic, Vedantist, or Buddhist, turns religion into a kind of compulsive poetry—poetry with an imperative attached. (I might point out that sometimes it isn't very well attached.)

The real reason for the popularity of the Occult Ancient East was pointed out long ago by Kipling: "Ship me somewhere East of Suez . . . where there ain't no ten commandments . . ." If your religion is just exotic enough, you don't need to bother about responsibility. You can get away with anything. There is nothing of this in Buber. For him the faith is the faith of his fathers, and the highest expression of that faith is its prayer, and prayer is the highest form of responsibility, the ultimately committed dialogue. This is an aesthetic statement, not a religious one, and in the final analysis all of Buber's major works are works of art. *I and Thou* is one of the greatest prose poems, an *Isaiah,* and a *Song of Myself.*

From *I and Thou* to his latest collection of essays, all of Martin Buber's work has been a celebration of the joys of communion. Will Herberg has recently included him in his collection, *Five Existentialist Theologians.* Now when Will Herberg was young and giddy and a Marxist, he had the reputation of being the only American of that persuasion whom the Kremlin ever took seriously as a thinker. He once wrote a pamphlet which I still treasure, called *The Stalinist Position on the American Negro,* which pretty well disposed of *that* folly forever. As he has grown older and got religion, he seems to have lost his sense of discrimination. "Existentialism" may be a fashionable term that helps sell books, but Martin Buber's connection with Existentialism is of the simplest and most fundamental kind—he is against it, and he has written more cogent polemic against it than anybody else who has ever bothered with it. He is the leading anti-Existentialist amongst modern religious writers. Maritain, one of the five, is neither a theologian nor an Existentialist. He is a religious journalist with a keen nose for catchwords that sell books.

Religious Existentialism descends directly from Augustine to Luther to Kierkegaard to Barth. It is obsessed with the absolute transcendence of the creator and the utter contingency of the creature, and it recognizes no mediation except a sort of historically instantaneous thunderbolt, the Incarnation of Jesus Christ, which must be accepted as an act of blind faith. It has no use for the responsibilities of community: Augustine put aside his wife, married after the rites of a slightly different sect, as a whore, and Kierkegaard's love life was a pitiable farce. It pictures man as ridden by the anxieties and terrors of his only spiritual ability—his realization of his own insignificance. This is why atheist Existentialism is a philosophy of despair, "the philosophy of the world-in-concentration-camp," a kind of utterly thoroughgoing masochism. Take away God and there is absolutely nothing left. Nothing but black bile. Nobody there. However Martin Buber might disagree doctrinally, take away his God and nothing important in his philosophy has changed. It remains a philosophy of joy, lived in a world full of others.

Actually, Buber's philosophy, technically speaking, is much like that of the English Hegelians, especially McTeggart, and the great forgotten American, Josiah Royce, just as his epistemology and his position in the Existentialist controversy is close to that of the contemporary English thinker, John Wisdom. The Beloved Community may not be for him, as a quasi-orthodox Jew, the Absolute, but it is the garment of the Absolute. And his epistemology is founded on the answer to the question "What is out there?" —"Other minds." And that answer is the title of John Wisdom's most seminal book. I am well aware that Buber's philosophical writings are an integral part of the modern Existentialist dispute. *Between Man and Man* is concerned almost entirely with the question of personality, the person as human being, the person as a member of society, the absolute personality. As such, written in Germany in the second quarter of this century, it is perforce a running commentary on Kierkegaard, Husserl, Heidegger, Scheler. But this does not make Buber an Existentialist any more than Aquinas is a Nominalist or an Averroist. Again, the American lectures gathered as *The Eclipse of God*, deal with God as absolute person and man as contingent. This is the favorite stamping ground of the Existentialists, and also, of course, American lectures must be about things up-to-date audiences want to hear.

Existentialism is a frame of mind. For people who do not know the maximum state of insecurity bred in most men caught in our disintegrating social fabric as in a thicket of fire, its dilemmas, like the epistemological dilemma that bothered the British for three centuries, simply do not exist. The dilemma does not exist for Buber. He cannot project himself with any success into the psychosis of total insecurity. He is too much at home in the world. Nothing shows this better than his treatment of Simone Weil in the essay, "The Silent Question" (from *At the Turning*), or of Sartre in *Eclipse of God*. Neither Weil nor Sartre is very great shakes as philosopher, but both are certainly pure Existentialist personalities, high-level Beatniks. Buber is very funny. Forced by popular demand to discuss an out-

113

rageous and pathetic girl, whose writings are a farrago of terror and misinformation, and a plain vulgar journalist, it is all he can do to control himself. His distaste for life lived on this level, for the most important issues exploited purely for sensationalism, for a kind of metaphysics of delinquency, is more than his sympathy can bear. He takes refuge from Simone Weil in his own orthodoxy. Sartre he dismisses with a compliment as a great literary artist. Coming from the author of *The Tales of the Hasidim* and *I and Thou*, this is the most ironic innocence.

He is so polite, this man with the most beautiful beard since von Hugel. He is so nice to Carl Jung. He picks his way so nicely, so kindly through and over the *disjecta membra* of that beached whale, the chubby corpse of Mme. Blavatsky, which is the gnostic theosophy of Jung, and even after Jung "answers" him in a half-cocked polemic full of pleas about the "science of psychology" from one of the most unscientific minds of all time, Buber so gently points out that the controversy is beneath the level of a second-year student in a good theological seminary—any time in the past fifteen hundred years. He does this, of course, purely by implication. Jung, I am sure, was completely unaware that he was thoroughly told off. Buber likes people. Had he met Simone Weil in person, he would have liked her, and it is a pity he didn't, because, had she listened, he would have done her a lot of good. Many girls and young men exactly like her must have come to him down the years. He is the kind of man whom any person in trouble would recognize on sight, or on the sight of a single book of his work, as the ideal confessor. Simone Weil did not like such people and avoided them. To her, they were what her more vulgar sisters call "the fuzz," representatives of her "Great Beast," the Social Lie.

Is Buber in any sense a representative of the Social Lie? Max Weber long ago pointed out that the use of a transcendental ideology to justify the betrayals and compromises of politics and economics is the essential social falsehood. The oncoming war is not going to be fought on either side for any sort of values whatsoever, and anybody who says it is is a liar or a dupe. We have finally reached a point where the very conditions under which they operate expose the fiction of politics and economics for what they are. If Buber were a spokesman for Judaism, or any other religion as an institution, or for Israel or any other State, then of course Simone Weil would be right.

This brings us at last to the meat and crux and essence of Buber's thought, his idea of community, his interpretation of the vocation of prophet, and hence, by implication, of his own social role vis-à-vis Hasidism. Buber's Existentialism is terminological—an accident of current talk; his Hasidism is at his heart. Now Buber's Hasidism is a very special thing, and for those who know nothing about the subject, his presentation can be not just very, but almost totally misleading. That is, for anybody seeking ordinary information. He has, practically singlehandedly, brought Hasidism to life for educated people. (The actual sect is still very much alive, especially among poorer Jews in, for instance, Williamsburg, Brooklyn.) But he has revivified only certain elements of this Jewish sect; much, in fact what most actual Hasids would have considered the most important parts, he has left dead and forgotten or has subtly reinterpreted. What is Hasidism—not Buber's Hasidism, but the historical movement as it appears in the record?

Hasidism is an ecstatic religious movement which resulted from the impact of popular Kabbalism on the folk culture of the eighteenth-century Polish ghetto. Many elements went to produce it. In part it was a pressure phenomenon like the pentecostal religions of the American Negro. Polish Jewish life in the eighteenth century was especially hard. The Messianic movement of Sabatei Zevi collapsed in spiritual demoralization when he became a Muslim. The partition of Poland subjected the Jewish communities to new problems. Life was insecure and unstable and full of disabilities and petty annoyances. Pogroms and persecutions increased. The community was driven in upon itself more than ever before, but it was driven in upon a specially rich folk culture, some of which was ancient, some of which was Russian or Polish in origin, some of which had developed *in situ*. All those folkways which one's Polish Jewish friends reminisce about with such gusto gave life in the ghetto and in the Jewish villages an intensity unlike anything in the peasant cultures of Western Europe. At the same time similar pentecostal and charismatic movements were sweeping through the Christian peasant communities of that part of the world. This was a time of great proliferation of the sects of Russian Dissenters, and of the East-ward movement of German Mennonites, Anabaptists, and Pietists.

Jews have been in Poland longer than anyone knows. The Persians settled Jewish communities on their northern borders beyond the Black Sea. The Khazar kingdom, Jew-ish in religion, competed with the Vikings, A.D. 600–800, for control of the waterways and the fur and amber trade of what is now Russia. In the Dark Ages the Jews were *voyageurs* much like the fur traders of French Canada cen-turies later, over all the Baltic-Black Sea river connections. These Jews were not Talmudists, and remnants of them still survive as Karaites—non-Talmudic Jews—in the Crimea and elsewhere.

Into the same borderlands, the Byzantine Empire had for centuries expelled incorrigible heretics. First the Pauli-cians and Gnostics, later the Bogomils. At one time much of the South Slav world was ruled by Bogomil dynasties. From the Bogomils by direct propaganda came the Cathari —the Albigenses of Provence. Russian dissent is strongly influenced by Bogomilism. Any unprejudiced study of Hasidism immediately reveals all sorts of ideas shared with Catharism.

Kabbalism dates back into the most obscure past of Judaism. It claims to be at least as old as Jewish orthodoxy, and it may well be right, but its basic document, *The Zohar*, was written in Spain in the Middle Ages. It is simply Jew-ish Gnosticism. This is disputed but it is none the less true. It shares every important feature with all the leading

**117**

Gnostic sects. From the inscrutable Godhead, Ayn Soph, emanate ten *sephiroth*, with names like Rigor and Mercy, the aeons of Valentinian. The final one, Malkuth, the Queen, is the physical manifestation of Deity in the universe. This is the Wisdom that danced before Him before the beginning of days, of the Book of Proverbs, the Shekinah, the Glory that hovered over the Ark and blessed with her presence all the great rites of passage and the festivals of the year. She is thought of as a hypostasis, a Divine Woman, the Bride of God, exactly like the Shakti of Shiva. She is also the abomination of desolation against whom the prophets continuously cry out. Ishtar, Astarte, Ashtoreth, the Baalat of Baal, the most ancient Canaanite goddess reasserts herself in eighteenth-century Poland.

A great deal of Kabbalism is taken up with alphabetical magic, and the manipulation of Biblical texts, numerologically and otherwise, to make them mean something quite different from what they say. Finally, the "innermost secrets" of the Kabbalah are what are occult in all occultism, various autonomic nervous system gymnastics of the sort we identify with Yoga, and erotic mysticism. For the Kabbalist the ultimate sacrament is the sexual act, carefully organized and sustained as the most perfect mystical trance. Over the marriage bed hovers the Shekinah. The Glory of God is revealed in the most holy of duties, and new souls are reborn into the sacred community of Israel. There are other notions—reincarnation, light metaphysics, worship of the planets and the moon, the latter identified with the Shekinah. (When Hasids dance in the public parks

118

of New York under the new moon with their hands over their heads, they are showing her her stigmata, found in the lunes of their fingernails, and celebrating her as their Great Mother.)

Kabbalism is thus one with the most ancient heterodoxy, and it well may be more ancient than any orthodoxy. Emanationism and some other doctrines are set forth in the so-called Memphite Theology, an Egyptian tractate older than the days of Moses and the Exodus. Kabbalism differs little from any other form of Gnosticism, whether of Kobo Daishi or Bardesanes, and as a full-fledged system it is certainly a few centuries older than the Christian Era. People who know of all this only through modern cultists or occult Freemasonry are under the impression that it was all thought up a couple of generations ago by Eliphas Levi and Mme. Blavatsky. On the contrary, its claims to antiquity are quite valid. There is one important particular in which Kabbalism differs from many Gnosticisms, and especially from Manichaeanism-Paulicianism-Bogomilism-Catharism. It is not dualistic. The final source of all reality is One, a hidden and unknowable God. Evil is explained in the various orthodox fashions—as a term of creation, as a manifestation of the recalcitrance of matter, as the result of a Fall, the Fall of the Angels and the Exile of the Shekinah, of Adam, and a falling apart of the manifest and the transcendent worlds, and finally—a notion shared with Indian Tantrism—as the "shells" left over, like burst vessels, from previous creations. The Biblical epic, from Abraham to the closing of the canon and on to the Fall of the Temple is considered to be the essential process of the return of the *sephiroth*. Hovering above the Torah, the Rite and the Law, the Shekinah is wed, the Creative Act is a closed circuit. Outside the Covenant or in the Diaspora, she is still in Exile. The Community of Israel *is* the Bride of Jehovah.

It must be pointed out that the various sects descended from Manichaeanism have all disclaimed dualism. The accusation comes from the orthodox. All this is repeated in the mystical doctrine of the Blessed Virgin—the names in the Litany of the BVM, the etherealization of the Song of Songs and the Books of Esther and Ruth, are common to Kabbalah and Mariolatry. For this reason and similar ones, conventional Jews have always been suspicious of Kabbalah as a transmission belt to Christianity. It has been so in the past and the leading twentieth-century Kabbalist, Paul Levertoff, became an Anglo-Catholic priest.

This is very heady stuff. History has proved, time and again, that when it gets out amongst the masses it can be extremely intoxicating and subversive of all decent social order. Except, reputedly, for the ancient Babylonian city of Harran, the last outpost of paganism to survive, and possibly for the Assassin inner community of Alamut, there has never been a stable polity reared on Gnosticism. The Kabbalists kept their speculations carefully confined to a very small elite. Much of the present *Prayerbook* is the work of one of the greatest Kabbalists that ever lived, but not one Jew in ten thousand is aware of it. Rabbi Israel ben **Eliezer Baal-Shem**, the founder of Hasidism, turned it into a popular cult, with an extremely active propaganda. He gave it a kind of organization. He imbedded it in the Yiddish folk culture. He did much more than this. He gave it an ethical content of a sort we do not know to have existed in any other Gnostic movement. Again, we know the ethical aspects of heresy only from the polemics of the orthodox. If Albigensian Provence, with all its wealth and culture, was anything like the poor villages of Poland gripped in the enthusiasm of the Hasidic movement, Europe was dealt a deadly blow by the Albigensian Crusade. Simon de Montfort and the Pope, Hitler and Himmler—perhaps there is something about the rage of the Great Beast at the sight of the pure joy of living which can be appeased only with the savor of burning human flesh.

Hasidism came to have a whole group ritual, special ways of celebrating the old Jewish holidays and rites of passage. Most conspicuous was ecstatic dancing of a peculiar character. It is like nothing else in the world, although I suppose its antecedents go back to the dancing dervishes of the Levant and through them to the Corybantic brotherhoods of the Baals and Baalats of Canaan. Great emphasis was placed on the bath of purification. For the antiquity of this we have physical evidence amongst the Essenes of the Dead Sea settlement. The Baal Shem frowned on asceticism and taught that the holy man "redeems" food and drink by consuming it. Alcohol was consumed, especially before dancing, to produce a kind of holy intoxication. Erotic mysticism and direct adoration of the Shekinah as the Bride of God were central to most

121

rites. The ritual dance was customarily performed to singing in which all took part, dancing in a circle around a
young boy with a pure unchanged voice who stood in the
center of the ring dance on a table, and who was understood
as a surrogate for a woman. Dances like this are referred
to in both the Jewish and the Christian Apocrypha and they
are common in other Gnostic sects from Japan to Bengal.
This, however, did not result in any sort of orgiastic sexual
promiscuity. There is no question but that sacred prostitutes, male and female, were part of the temple ritual until
the revolution which "discovered the ancient documents"
of the present Torah. In Hasidism their place is taken by
each married couple—a temple unto themselves. All
Hasidim, and especially their leaders, the Zaddiks, were
expected to marry, and the final expression of erotic mysticism was centered in the marriage bed and the family. In
this way Hasidism, after all its colorful and emotional de-
tour, returns to be at one with the most orthodox mystery
of Judaism—the seed of Israel.

Hasidism was organized exactly like the Albigenses.
There was an elite, called Zaddiks, which means the Right-
eous, corresponding to the elite of the Albigenses, the
Cathari or Purified Ones. They were usually rabbis, but
not always, and like the imams of the Shi'ite Muslims,
there were supposed to be always thirty-six Hidden Zaddiks, or sometimes only one who was a sort of bodhisattva
or latent Messiah, and from whom flowed the holiness of the
others. Around each of these especially devoted and illuminated leaders (they were thought of, like the Cathari, as

literally filled with light) were grouped little fellowships of the rank and file Hasidim, an ecstatic, dancing, singing, gesticulating band who greatly resemble the first Franciscans and may well have resembled in actual behavior the first disciples of Christ (who, we may be sure, did *not* comport themselves like the Bench of Bishops).

The Zaddiks were direct sources of *mana,* holy power, which could be tapped by less saintly laymen, and they were equally direct advocates with God. To each Zaddik the laity brought little slips of paper inscribed with all the troubled petitions of life and with the petitioner's name and, not his father's, as is the Jewish custom, but with his mother's name. The Zaddiks spent long hours in meditative prayer, in the course of which all the day's petitions were presented before the Throne of Mercy. If this constitutes the essence of priesthood the Zaddikkim were priests, and as such the only priesthood surviving in Jewry outside of the Falasha of Abyssinia. In the course of time this custom and another like it, which greatly resembled the sale of indulgences that disgraced Renaissance Roman Catholicism, came to corrupt Hasidism, and many Zaddiks ended up rich, vain, drunken exploiters of ignorant slum and village superstition. The Hasidic community was a genuine fellowship. The laity spent a great deal of time with their masters, in the synagogues and schools, and at table, eating with them if possible on all the holidays and on every Sabbath, especially the third Sabbath meal—the Feast of the Queen. Alcohol, dance, song, sex all played a part, but above all else, Hasidism was a *religion of conversation.* In this, once

123

again, it must have been very like the earliest days of Christianity. The Marriage Feast at Cana, the Miracle of the Loaves and Fishes, the Last Supper—these are all intensely Hasidic episodes.

This special temper seems to have been always latent in Jewry and in eighteenth-century Poland the Hasidic propaganda fell on fertile soil. Almost everything which the non-religious American treasures as part of the Jewish contribution to modern culture comes from the intense and intensely gregarious life of the Polish ghetto. Above all else it is a frame of mind, an insouciance in the face of the cruel absurdities of life, a very special kind of whimsical irony, which has passed over, emasculated, to become our typical modern American (*New Yorker*) humor, an inexhaustible, mocking fantasy, a special kind of intimacy which is compounded of a general ebullient love of man and of life and a very active interest in the immediate partner of any dialogue. This is the Hasidic temper. It gives the characteristic color to those typical Jewish jokes and anecdotes which are so much funnier than other jokes. From it come all the great Yiddish writers, from Sholem Aleichem to Moishe Nadir, the visionary poets like Yehoash. It gives the Yiddish theater its effervescence and poignancy. Zak, Zakkine, Soutine, many Americans—my friends Doner and Zakheim amongst them—these are all Hasidic artists, and the greatest of all, of course, the pure illustrator of the Hasidic spirit, is Marc Chagall, whose paintings find their parallel in *The Tales of the Hasidim* of Buber. The intended canard of chauvinists that jazz is Negro and Jewish music is perfectly correct. It is the ecstatic Hasidic heritage that made it possible for American musicians from Avenue A and Maxwell Street and Williamsburg to meet the Negro half way.

The Hasidic movement at its height included close to half the population of Jewish Poland. What effect did such an explosion have on the orthodox? Surprisingly little, considering. In the first place, Kabbalism as long as it was veiled in the decent obscurity of learning was a perfectly respectable part of Judaism. In the second place, all their opponents, the *mitgnagdim*, shared the same folk culture, unless they were assimilated—renegades—a good deal worse than being Hasids. Many of the doctrines and ideas and practices of the Hasidim were paralleled in the regular Jewish community. The Hasidic movement just gave them a new emotional content and so shaped them to a more ecstatic form. Eventually many of the Zaddikkim became very learned, with a rather crazy kind of learning, and were able to dispute the rabbis on their own ground, and the power of learning, Jewish learning, is respected by even the most bigoted.

And then, finally, there is no Jewish orthodoxy in the sense a Christian would understand. It is possible to believe in heaven, hell, and purgatory, or in reincarnation, or in no after life at all, and still be a good Jew. The emanationism and hypostases of Kabbalah have never been challenged as either polytheism or pantheism. It is inconceivable that the world of Jewry could ever tear itself asunder over speculations as to the exact nature of subtle psychological processes in the structure of the Deity, or as to the exact nature and occasion of God's saving grace. If you preserve the unity of the Godhead and keep the Torah, you are a Jew and no rabbi, however learned, can say you nay. The Jews are the only people who have ever met the supposed threat of a widespread movement of the Gnostic type without persecution to the point of extermination. True, *mitgnagdim* means "persecutors"—but the defensive measures of the conventional communities of Poland were affectionate compared with the Albigensian Crusade, the Persian crusade against Mani—and in our own day against the Bahai movement, or the Lutheran suppression of the Anabaptists of the Munster Commonwealth. In fact, all Judaism, from Frankfort to Jerusalem, from Lithuania to Rumania, felt the influence of the Hasidic movement and shows it to this day. (There exists another province of Hasidism, the popular Kabbalism of Levantine and Sephardic Jews. It had demonstrable connections with the movement of Baal Shem Tov but it is not important in a consideration of Martin Buber's neo-Hasidism.) Hasidism itself is still very much alive and typical Hasidim can be seen any day—but the Sabbath—by anyone who cares to visit the fur district of New York at lunch hour. It is not only powerful in Israel, but its rites and ceremonies with their dancing and songs and joy of life are the direct source of the folk customs of the neo-Judaism of the *kibbutzim*, the Jewish cooperative communes in Israel. The "Israeli" songs and dances that have become so popular a part of the Zionist propaganda in America and that can be heard at parties of the most sophisticated Jewish young people are Hasidic, not Palestinian, in origin.

Hasidism owes its power and durability to its ethical content, and to the specific kind of ethical content. Partly this is simply Jewish, but much of it is the teaching of the Baal Shem and his first disciples. There have been lots of Baal Shems; the term means the "master of the name," a Kabbalist who has discovered or inherited one of the secret names of God and can work magic with it and summon up powers and demons. Baal Shem Tov, as Rabbi Eliezer was called, is the master of the Good Name, the Kabbalist who can work miracles in the souls of men. Actually, Baal Shem Tov seems to have been an almost illiterate man as far as Kabbalistic learning went, and many of the early Zaddikkim were simple workmen, woodcutters, coachmen, potters, butchers, tanners—many of them from occupations of dubious purity from the strict Jewish point of view. Hasidism is ethical mysticism. Its dominant characteristic is joy in the good—in the good in every sense of the word, in life, in the good things of life, in the beauty of creation, in the good in all men, and in doing good. The joke, "Good food, good drink, good God, let's eat," could well be a brief Hasidic "grace."

The great trouble with Talmudic Judaism is that it was used up emotionally—it had become a religion of rules and prescriptions, very difficult to get excited about. Hasidism changed all this. The Torah, the Law, became a source of endless intoxicating joy. To use the vulgar phrase of a bad American revivalist, they discovered that it was fun

127

to do good and to be good. It is curious that with the exception of the Quakers, Christianity and the religions influenced by it teach or at least imply that it is very, very hard
to be a good human being. This is simply not true, not at
least for a person uncorrupted by manufactured guilts. It
is not only easy to avoid lying, stealing, fornication, covetousness, idolatry, lust, pride, anger, jealousy, and the rest,
it is a positive pleasure. Essential to such a life are magnanimity, courage, and the love and trust of other men.
These are above all others the Hasidic virtues, along with
humility, simplicity, and joy. These are all virtues of direct
dealing with other men—the virtues of dialogue. To the
Hasid the mystical trance is a dialogue. The self does not
unself itself, but "forgets itself" in conversation with the
Other; and from the Other, i.e., God as the ultimate and
perfect partner of dialogue, flows out the conversation with
all others—the life of dialogue, the philosophy of Martin
Buber.

What Buber has done is divest Hasidism of its Gnosticism, and of the extremities and eccentricities of conduct
which are the marks of isolated sectarianism. Unless he
himself has some personal esoterism he has not divulged to
us, he has discarded all of its occult lore and practice. What
he has kept is the folk spirit, the ethical gospel, and above
all the specific temper. Baron von Hugel says somewhere
that one of the essential signs of sanctity in the process of
canonization is a certain pervasive sweetness of temper—a
kind of holy good humor—or possibly just plain good
humor. It is this *courtoisie* which Hasidism shares with the

early Franciscans and which is so rare a virtue amongst the professedly religious. Least of all is it common amongst the Romantic Traditionalists, the inventors and followers of our modern archaizing neo-religions. Let a contemporary intellectual start reading Thomas Aquinas or Dr. Suzuki and he immediately adopts all those lovely virtues preached by Christ or Buddha—pride, arrogance, intolerance, bigotry, ill temper, anger. It is not for nothing that the Pope condemned *L'Action Française*. It was a parade of all the deadly sins in literary guise—in the guise of Catholic polemic and apologetic. Von Hugel of course was not a convert, he was a born Catholic of great power and influence; he rather was trying to convert the Church. Possibly Buber is in the same position. He has taken a movement of ghetto, slum, and peasant enthusiasts of which most educated Jews were secretly ashamed, and has used it to reform, restate, and give new emotional meaning to what he considers to be the essence of Judaism. It is quaint to notice that his American exponent, Will Herberg, is still embarrassed by the ruffianly antecedents of Buber's philosophy and tries as best he can to ignore his Hasidism altogether and to make him out a fashionable existentialist. You can get a far more reliable picture of Buber as man and thinker from Maurice Friedman, to whom Buber's Hasidism is central and paramount.

*I and Thou*—the life of dialogue. We have heard something like this from that most bankrupt of all sectarian sects, American Liberal Protestantism (or Reformed Judaism). Does this mean "sharing," folksiness, "group dynamics"? I know of no more obnoxious experience than to be approached after a lecture or reading by some ass in well-shined face and well-shined shoes who says, "I'd like to share your thinking about Red China—or Birth Control—or Juvenile Delinquency." Who is he to ask a piece of my mind for a piece of his? At this moment America is bedeviled by the popinjays of Togetherness. Recently my little daughter came home from school and asked for twenty-five cents for her Good Citizen Milk. Anybody who, at this stage of the game, starts talking about this subject is treading on dangerous ground and should rightly be viewed with the greatest suspicion. What sort of dialogue is this? Certainly our current Togetherness is simply the massing of frightened ciphers and only adds up to a compulsory vacuum.

This of course is not Buber's notion. For him the reciprocal response I and Thou is the only mode of realization of the fullest potential of each party. The one realizes itself by realizing the other. *The ego is by definition the capacity to respond.* It does not lie in some inner recess of the person, but is "out there," it is built in the fullness of our intercourse with others. We respond to a person, we react to things. True, a great deal of our relations with other men is systems of reaction, but *morality is the art of substituting response for reaction.* In so far as another human being is treated as a thing he is dehumanized. This is not a new concept. We have heard the term "reification" before, here in America. Conversely, Buber says somewhere that all things come to us as more or less manifest or remote perspectives on persons, and this, certainly, is pure British Hegelian Idealism of fifty years ago. In fact, it is pure McTeggart. "All real living is meeting," says Buber.

"Pure," "Absolute," "Ideal"—such a philosophy deals in the most transcendent material and therefore, as it presents itself in the world, must show its *bona fides*. We have been far more than twice burned and the baby goes reluctantly back to the candle. McTeggart's philosophy of love led him to demand the expulsion of Bertrand Russell from his university because he was a conscientious objector, on humane grounds, to the least justifiable war in history. How much is Buber open to the accusation of Max Weber?

It is possible to put together an irreproachable catena of quotations on all the crucial questions of our violently sick social order. The community emerges out of the I-Thou relation, not conversely. "Only men capable of truly saying Thou to one another can truly say We with each other." "Individualism understands only a part of man, collectivism understands man only as a part; neither advances to the wholeness of man. Individualism sees man only in relation to himself, but collectivism does not see man at all; it sees 'society.' Individuation is a reciprocal process and hence cannot exist in autonomy. There is nothing to confirm." "Confirmation of the self through the collective is pure fiction."

Against individualism and collectivism, Buber advocates communism—that communism with a small "c" which is almost forgotten today. His ideas can be paralleled in dozens of "communitarian" writers, from the socialists

Engels dismissed as "Utopian" to Bakunin, Kropotkin, the Russian Socialist-Revolutionaries, Berkman, Gorter, as well as some Roman Catholic radical social thinkers. All of these people envisaged their communities as coming about after either an overthrow of the existing society or in isolation after a total turning away, geographically as well as physically and morally, from our own moribund competitive society. Buber identifies his communitarian ideal with the actually existing *kibbutzim* in modern Israel. Now these are, most of them, committed to a peculiarly unreal Bolshevism-without-the-Bolsheviks of their own, a kind of etherealized Stalinism. Others are religious communities of various states of orthodoxy. They are quasi-military in their internal life. All basic relationships and duties are compulsory. They are directly military in their external relations. Most of them are armed outposts, constantly on the defense against Arab invasion or infiltration. *They are almost completely devoid of privacy*. The I-Thou relation requires that the parties have an always open opportunity to be alone together. This simply is not permitted in the typical *kibbutz*. They are, of course, part of the state policy of the aggressive State of Israel. They are the perfected fulfillment of the "movement"—a depersonalizing thing of delegated responsibility, of ideological command and obedience, of Zionism. Finally, without a continuing stream of American money, from Jews still deeply committed to competitive individualism and patriotic collectivism, they would not exist at all.

Buber tries hard to etherealize both the Zionist movement and the State of Israel. He considers this the redemptive role of prophecy, the continual confrontation of the secular state with the transcendental demands of an intention, a destination, beyond the world. This may give him comfort, but it does not alter the facts. Zionism remains an imperialist maneuver, invented by Napoleon and taken over by the British and used with considerable effectiveness in the First World War. Israel remains the final outcome of this maneuver, an aggressive nationalist State founded on invasion and war, and perpetuated by conscription of both girls and boys and by the militarization of wide sections of life. In New York the Hasidim of Williamsburg rioted against the conscription of women.

We have dozens of articles and speeches of Buber's, first to Zionist meetings and conferences, later to groups in the State of Israel. Again and again he stresses the responsibility of the Jews as the chosen people to redeem the world, and he states specifically that to do this, to even begin to do it—to be a chosen people in the full sense of the word—the Jews must have a "homeland," a nation with a political structure of power and discipline and a geographic location—Palestine. Of course the notion of a chosen people is a foolish and dangerous superstition which has caused untold harm in the world. If a chosen people, say the Mormons or the Jehovah's Witnesses, are utterly without real temporal power, it is possible to etherealize this calling into a spiritual vocation. But it is not possible to etherealize actual temporal power. You cannot etherealize the State of Israel any more than you can etherealize the Vatican or the

Kremlin. All three are actually there, they are not rash ideas but concrete physical masses of political power. And if you go back to the foundations of Buber's philosophy and religion, and go logically from there to the question of political power, to the nation and the State, it is all too apparent that they are evil as such, the manifest contradiction of the basic principles of his morality.

Israel he tries to etherealize by equating it with the Israel of the Old Testament. This is the people with whom the Lord swore a covenant. This is the people Moses led out of Egypt as the deputy of God. Buber's political and social writings are full of appeals to Biblical religion and to the personality of Moses. This is strange talk for a neo-Hasid. The great stumbling block for all Gnosticism has always been the Old Testament. Many Christian Gnostic sects held that it was written by the Devil. Certainly Kabbalah is nothing more nor less than an elaborate device to juggle the plain words of the Biblical narrative and make them mean the opposite of what they all too obviously do mean.

It is rather late in the day to have to recall that the Old Testament is one of the most disagreeable books in all the unpleasant history of religion. The Children of Israel are no better and no worse than the Children of Egypt or the Children of Athens. They are simply vain, foolish, and irresponsible, a prey to rumor and appetite, and always ready to let go a greater ultimate good for any immediate satisfaction. But their God is another matter. He is vindictive, jealous, angry, bloodthirsty, given to the tantrums of a child, and so thoroughly dishonest that he did not dare include "Thou shalt not lie" amongst his own ten commandments. The story of the invasion of Canaan is no more bloody and unscrupulous than any other tale of conquest, but the narrator is insufferably self-righteous about it. The early Gnostics were perfectly right. What the Old Testament teaches is not virtue but "sin," murder, adultery, deception, anger, jealousy, above all, *disloyalty*, Buber's primary sin. No other sacred book is so utterly immoral.

Buber stresses over and over again that Jehovah reveals himself to the Jews in history, that Judaism is a religion of historical revelation. It is precisely for this reason that its god is such a wretched creature. "God" does not work in history, man works in history. If God is the sum total of being viewed as a "Thou," this sum total is always frivolous. This is why the *Iliad* is so superior to the Old Testament. The universe and its separate great natural forces are neither good nor bad, but over against the works of men they are always senseless. The virtues, all the enduring values of life are products of the transient associations of mortal men—they are the heroes, and the proper attitude of a virtuous man towards the universe viewed as a whole is that it is dangerous. Viewed as a person, it is a fool. Buber goes back always to the Song of Deborah, presumably because it is the oldest of the documents of the Old Testament. It is an exciting poem, but a people who persist in believing that the stars in their courses fight for them is nothing but a nuisance and a menace. The stars in their courses do not fight, they burn, and eventually they burn out. The Heroic Age produces moving poetry, but a people

135

who believes in its own heroic epics does so not just at its peril, but at the peril of everybody else.

Buber's *Moses* is a curious document. It is his attempt to etherealize the most obnoxious part of the Old Testament narrative. He throws overboard at the beginning all the results of two centuries of Biblical criticism as beside the point and strives to return to what the experience of Exodus meant immediately to the participants. He then proceeds to pick and choose from the very textual, anthropological, and historical research he has discarded and to construct a narrative and a personality of Moses to suit himself. What emerges is simply a self-portrait, a kind of symbolic autobiography. In a footnote he regrets the rash and ill-informed Moses book of Freud's, but his is no different. It is better, yes, but because Buber is a far better man than Freud, not for any reasons connected with the text, Moses, or the wanderings of the Children of Israel.

It is pitiful to watch a man of Buber's intelligence and goodness struggling in the toils of an outworn and abandoned social paranoia. For thousands of years men of good will have been trying to make Judaism and Christianity morally palatable to sane and civilized men. No other religions have ever required such efforts at etherealization. Today we think of Islam as a rather elementary and provincial religion—or at least of the *Koran* as such a book. But we forget, confused by centuries of misleading apologetics, what an enormous advance over both Christianity and Judaism Islam was. Why do people bother? If they must have a religion, the basic texts of Taoism, Buddhism,

Confucianism need no such reworking. It may be necessary, particularly of the Buddhist documents, to trim off
the exotic rhetoric, but it is not necessary to make them
mean exactly the opposite of what they say.

Buber does not succeed as well as the Kabbalists and
Hasidim before him. Neither Moses nor Jehovah was an
enlightened, humane unitarian and socialist of the Weimar
Republic. There is only one kind of writer that we can
afford to forgive for such willful perversions of history
and present fact, especially in spiritual matters, and that
is an artist. If we lay aside all Buber's pretensions as theologian and religious leader, we are left with him as poet.
*I and Thou, Tales of the Hasidim, For the Sake of Heaven*
—we can judge these as works of art, as symbolic criticism
of value, as works of spiritual insight with their kind of
veracity. Even here there are limits. We can forgive Dante
for a narrow vindictive mind of shocking cruelty, very like
his Old Testament god, by the way. We can, if we confine
ourselves to the two great novels, forgive Céline for being
an anti-Semite, but when, as the Communists used to say,
"Art is a weapon," then we cannot forgive. We cannot forgive the direct, depraved political tendentiousness of T. S.
Eliot, Ezra Pound, or Guillevic.

The religion of the Old Testament is morally obnoxious
in the extreme. Does Buber as artist preach it? Of course
he does not. There is no empiric justification for the logical
drive toward simplification and concentration that leads to
monotheism. Entities are multiplied without sufficient reason. The universe is not orderly in the same way as the

137

mind of man. Only as a concept is nature a unity. Is this monotheistic deity, dredged up from the shores of the Red Sea out of the midst of a petty battle—is he essential to the understanding of these works as works of art? Certainly not. Behind all the ontological confabulation into which Buber's enthusiasm and the weight of his tradition drive him is a simple response to the most ordinary fact of life—the presence of other persons and the possibility of love.

*I and Thou* is a sort of Rochester in reverse. As Rochester's poems are typical seventeenth-century hymns in which the name of the Deity has been replaced by the name of his mistress, Buber's wonder and excitement at the discovery of love in a loveless world, his astonishment that there is another "out there," mount steadily to such a pitch that by the second half of the book no human object can contain the burden of awe and ecstasy. Love is essentially a relationship—it and its parties are relative, contingent, it is this which gives it its pathos. At the end of a long life, the husband of one woman, the Japanese poet says, "We thought our love would last a thousand years, and we were together only a little while." Love can be made the final value, or the most important one in the shifting and flowing of contingency, but if too great a burden is placed on it, any vehicle must break down. The contingent collapses into the absolute. The wine overflows the vessel and shatters it and spills into the sea. But the sea is not a person. "Being as a whole viewed as a Thou" self-evidently is a product of insatiable desire, not of any evidence at all. We are familiar with these love poems—Richard Rolle, Julian of Norwich,

The Cloud of Unknowing, John Ruysbroeck, Walter Hilton —the beautiful but insatiable lust no earthly lover can satisfy. But saying so does not make it true, any more than saying so makes Moses a liberal traditionalist or an ethical mystic of the twentieth century, or an armed *kibbutz* a Brotherhood of Love. The pious who believe that if you just want something hard enough and pray for it hard enough you get it are alas, but fortunately, wrong. Voltaire to the contrary, no need is great enough to create an absolute satisfaction. Death perhaps, certainly nonexistence, is the only absolute man can imagine.

As a poem, *I and Thou* is very beautiful. But it is this metaphysical greed which removes it from the category of the highest art. There is amongst men no absolute need. The realization of this is what makes Homer and the Greek tragedians so much sounder a Bible than the Old or New Testaments. Love does not last forever, friends betray each other, beauty fades, the mighty stumble in blood and their cities burn. The ultimate values are love and friendship and courage and magnanimity and grace, but it is a narrow ultimate, and lasts only a little while, contingent on the instability of men and the whims of "Nature viewed as a Thou." Like life, it is Helen's tragedy that gives her her beauty or gives Achilles and Agamemnon their nobility. Any art which has a happy ending in reserve in Infinity is, just to that degree, cheating. It is, I think, this pursuit of the absolute, the Faustianism of Spengler, which vitiates most Western art. We feel embarrassed at Goethe's paeans to the Eternal Feminine as the conclusion of his pitiful drama.

Early in life Buber turned away from what he considered the self-obliterative mysticism of the East. But he was wrong. Taoism is not self-obliterative. In a sense it is not even mysticism. It is rather just a quiet and fairly accurate assessment of the facts. Perhaps the self which demands an Absolute Partner for its life of dialogue is obliterating itself, or at least crippling itself. It seems to me that the fullest realization of the self comes in the acceptance of the limits of contingency. It is harder, but more ennobling, to love a wife as another human being, fugitive as oneself, than it is to carry on imaginary conversations with an imaginary Absolute. The demand to be loved totally, irrevocably, destroys first the love and then the lover. It is a kind of depersonalization—the opposite pole, but exactly like prostitution. It is this over-ambition which haunts all of Buber. Israel, Zion, "God"—these are all power concepts; they represent "success." But the real essence of Buber's philosophy has no place for success and no place for power. "Live unknown." "Own nothing you can't leave out in the rain." "Never think of men except in terms of those specific individuals whose names you know." These old saws are exemplified once more in his Hasidism. Why bother? They are so *easy* to act on, and the passion for power and success is so tiring, so depersonalizing.

I think this is the reason that the most fruitful social result of *I and Thou* is to be found not in religion, but in psychiatry. Buber's concepts and those of his followers

have given new life to the American schools of so-called
"interpersonal psychology." He is a far greater man than
any of the leaders of the Baltimore-Washington movement
—Adolph Meyer, William Alanson White, Harry Stack
Sullivan, Trigant Burrow. None of these men was a very
clear thinker and they were all very bad writers. They were
on the right track, but they expressed themselves abom-
inably. Now they are all dead and a group of younger men,
strongly influenced by Buber, are giving their concepts
new clarity and depth. Once again, as so often in dealing
with Buber's ideas, we return to the tradition of William
James.

*Tales of the Hasidim,* the books about Rabbi Nachman
and Baal Shem Tov, the novel, *For the Sake of Heaven,* are
hardly fiction at all, but collections of anecdotes of the
Hasidim. They are filled with joy, wonder, modesty, and
love. It is their own peculiar moral character which lifts
them above the general run of Oriental pious tales, whether
of Sufi or Shi'ite saints or of Chuang Tzu and Lieh Tzu and
the Taoist adepts. Now the remarkable thing about the
Hasidic response to the wonder of the world is that it im-
plies an unconscious but none the less enthusiastic acceptance of its contingency. God is there, as he is in *I and Thou,*
as a center and referrent, as the ultimate reduction, as the
repository of all excess demand—but what comes through
most is joy and wonder, love and quiet, in the face of the
continuously vanishing world. It is called God's Will, but
the movement of the universe—not from Infinity to Eter-
nity, but just endless—is accepted on very similar terms to

141

those of the *Tao Te Ching*. Song and dance, the mutual love of the community—these are the values; they are beautiful precisely because they are not absolute. And on this foundation of modesty and love and joy is raised a moral structure which heals and illuminates as hardly any other Western European religious expression does. "Heals and illuminates"—again we come back to the health which can be found only in a true community of true persons.

There are faults, not least of which is the careful expurgation of the erotic and intoxicated elements of Hasidism. The Shekinah herself is always referred to as "It," never as "She," whole realms of Hasidic practice and experience are quietly ignored. These are Buber's Hasidim, not the real seventeenth-century ones, and in this sense the books are fictions. But nowhere else does his philosophy come through with such poignant simplicity—or, for that matter, with such complexity. Not only does he face the actual complexities of real human relationships amongst individual men and women—rather than abstractions like "Israel" or "Zionism"—but many of the cryptic Kabbalistic sayings of the Zaddiks are given a kind of surrealist, symbolic burden, so that they function as little poems, illuminating experience in their own dark way. And finally, the morality, the ethics, the religion are all so much clearer in this living context. Nowhere is there a better criticism of the folly of using the transcendent to affect the mundane world of power politics than in *For the Sake of Heaven*. Buber has written his own best answer to his Zionism and nationalism.

# WAS IT THE CONGRESS
# OF VIENNA?

*The International Industrial Development Conference,*
*San Francisco, 1957*

Seven hundred capitalists is a lot of capitalists to see all at
once. But it is not as breathtaking as you might think. Coming suddenly out of the bright San Francisco sunshine into
the dim lobbies of the Fairmont Hotel, they don't look
much different from you and me. They are members of the
blue serge and grey flannel and pin stripe international,
just like the people in the corridors of the UN or in any
professional, technical, or administrative convention the
world over, including the other side of the Iron Curtain.
This has often been remarked in other contexts—but it is
a little startling to discover that it is true of what was once
the silk-hat, big-paunch, striped-pants, chorus-girl-on-knee
world of the *Masses* cartoonists. Alas, that gaudy show is
gone forever. They may run the world, but I can tell at a
glance that these boys are every bit as fouled-up as I am,
and lots of them may be almost as well educated. Until you
look at the badges, you can't tell Press from Guest, except
for the *Time-Life* people, who look as though they'd just
eaten the canary, and the Formosans. The condottieri of the
Nationalist Chinese regime are out of another age altogether, not that of the Robber Barons, but out of the slip-

143

pery back corridors of the Renaissance. They look like combinations of various proportions of Fu Manchu, the plumper Buddha statues, and Get Rich Quick Wallingford. Their air of fabulously expensive evil living lends a slight chill of distinction to an otherwise somewhat academic looking mob.

Seven hundred of the boys who run the world. I wonder if Wright Mills is right. Is it a conspiracy of mediocrity? Just as an amateur physiognomist I would hazard the guess that the IQ level was higher here than anywhere except in a gathering of top scientists. Most of them look smart, a few look like they really knew the score, and the Asians especially look like well-fed intellectuals. But they don't look like the Master Class, and very few look like Men of Distinction. I think people who do look like that, by and large, are male models, and mostly neither very bright nor very nice.

This thing started off as a quiet little gathering of a few industrialists, economists, bankers, and such, organized by the Stanford Research Institute. It probably wouldn't have amounted to much. And then Henry Luce offered to pick up the tab. So everybody wanted to come. As the call girl said, "San Francisco is the town where everybody wants to come to ball, baby." So there are bankers from Ceylon, cement manufacturers from Iran, Burmese mining magnates, Japanese economists, terribly flattered economics professors from everywhere, and a few of the really important lads from the real top, and one lady delegate, who makes pop in Siam and looks like a dangerous beauty from the pages of

Talbot Mundy. For a week she wears fur hats exclusively, made out of odd beasts like binturongs and dappled coypus. Nobody knows why she was invited, but what *Time* calls the "newshens" sure love her, and the assorted billionaires don't seem to mind her a bit. Such is Life; such, too, is Time.

Mr. Luce's first words are, "This is the fulfillment of a life-long dream." Yes, indeed, I know what he means. Imagine what would have happened if William Randolph Hearst, Sr., had tried to stage something like this. The poor man, the New York politicians didn't even dare sell him so socially undistinguished an honor as the mayoralty. But this is the day of the New Journalism, which is something like the New Capitalism. And they get along fine. Seven hundred people were flattered to be asked. And there is Henry the missionary's boy, on the platform speaking his piece for company, seven hundred cover stories in the flesh. It's lovely to see a man make good. It was a touching speech.

From then on, beginning with Eugene Black of the International Bank for Reconstruction, the speeches weren't touching at all. They were dismaying. There was nothing of Jim Fiske or Henry Clay Frick, nothing of a McCormick or Luce editorial in these papers. A lot of serious thought and hard work, by ghosts and, I suspect, in most cases by tycoons, too, had gone into them. But Black's paper sounded like a scolding from J. P. Morgan, Sr.'s parson. It was an ominous keynote, all about stability and reliability and a friendly and cooperative attitude on the part of the lesser

145

breeds and the dangers of socialism and nationalism. From then on it was turn and turn about. The earnest and immensely civilized brown men, bankers and millionaires and arch conservatives in their own countries, tried to explain what was happening in the world. Over and over again the seven hundred were told that in the have-not three quarters of the world the population is exploding, the standard of living is falling, capital accumulation lags far behind the most elementary needs, the old peasant economies are dead, dying, or demoralized; outside of part of Europe, the USA, Britain and her Dominions, and a few other places, the "free" world is turning into an immense slum. Not only is there more poverty than fifty years ago, but today the people of the "former" colonial nations are acutely aware of their poverty. They measure it against the luxurious life they see in the American movies, and unless something is done soon to increase their productive powers "there will be serious disturbances." And, again, that given this all-enveloping poverty, major capital investment can be undertaken only by the state; there are not even the human resources to handle it any other way.

Long ago someone said that Bolshevism was destined to be the characteristic political form assumed by the colonial and semi-colonial nations as they embarked on the course of primitive capital accumulation. The assumption was that it had only verbal connections with the socialism of the nineteenth-century imperialist powers, but was a socialization of poverty, the dragooning of a broken down peasant economy into industrialism. Recently even Earl Browder

146

has been saying something like this. And of course it is the "Marxism" implicit in Khrushchev's famous but somewhat "un-Marxist" speech to the Twentieth Party Congress. Well, if they have their way, the majority of the capitalists of Europe, assuming they were properly represented at this conference, are going to see to it that this is what happens. They just didn't pay any attention to what their brown and yellow colleagues were telling them. They drew a blank. They didn't dig it, like Eddie Condon listening to Stan Kenton. Nothing happened, man. Either they are all incorrigible or the wrong white men came. If this thing was designed to counteract Bandung, it laid an egg. One after another, Germans, Americans, British—it was the same old tale, very politely phrased by captive economics professors and *Time* style experts, but the same old refrain: "You little stinkers, show some gratitude and promise to be good or you won't get any candy." Some didn't even try to disguise it. Hermann J. Abs, the German banker, who looks as though he had worked hard, hard, all his life, trying to look like the Coldstream Guards, did all but call for gunboats to be sent to the coconut isles. He obviously had learned nothing and forgotten nothing—since the Herero War. It may have been Kitchener of Khartoum translated into high finance, but it certainly dismayed his colleague on the platform, the Filipino banker, Mr. Cuaderno.

So it went, day after day. The Asians were trying to defend capitalism—after all, they were all capitalists. And they were trying to tell their "former" imperialist masters the only way it could be done. They were very well-in-

147

formed, far better educated, far more men of the world. Most of their papers would not have looked too odd in the *Nation*. Many were trained at the London School of Economics. Except for very rare exceptions, mostly amongst the Americans, their listeners would have understood as much if they had spoken Etruscan.

There were exceptions. When the economists spoke under their own names, most of them tried to throw a scare into the boss. The boss just went to sleep or looked irritated— the egghead exposure syndrome. One or two, as might be expected, were real bawds, and gave pep talks worthy of a morning pow-wow of Fuller Brush salesmen. Paul Hoffman made a surprise appearance and spoke very intelligently. Many of the round table leaders and participants, the Americans especially, showed considerable insight. But by and large there was very much not a meeting of minds. Innate brains don't matter, not if they are blocked by incorrigible folly and invincible ignorance. I assume David Sarnoff has a lot of brains of some sort or he wouldn't be where he is, but he sounded like a supersalesman of electronically controlled, jet-propelled, lucite orange-squeezers.

The star of the show was M. R. Masani, one of India's leading conservatives. He explained once again the necessity for a "mixed economy": state socialism, cooperatives, village collectives, private enterprise, and foreign investment. And he ended, "May I take the liberty of suggesting that every American who invests in countries like mine is, whether he knows it or not, taking out an insurance policy for his children?" It certainly looked as though he might not. The American, Robert Garner, president of the International Finance Corporation, went blindly ahead with the same old scolding. All about "suspicion and hostility," "political nostrums," "the proven principles of free enterprise," in fact his reaction to the programs of economic development in the "former" colonial countries was "painful observance of political instability, disorderly national finances, inexperience in administrative management and techniques." And boys, if you don't mend your ways, don't come around my shop for any of my nice International Finance. Is it really happening? Or is it all a bad Russian propaganda movie? Sometimes I think that ten years back I wandered onto a Sovkino lot and I can't get out of the picture.

Still, these seven hundred fellows are all businessmen. They know nothing happens at conferences like this. History is made far more covertly today than it was in the days of Castlereagh and Talleyrand. What they came for was good hot business contacts, just like the delegates to any far less ambitious, far more Babbitt-attended business conference of plumbers or farm machinery salesmen. This they got and they were pleased and satisfied. The American lady from Siam should be able to go home and make a far more splendid pop for the Siamese.

What did it mean? Practically nothing. Seven hundred of the rulers of the world met. In another age they could have changed history. They got, at least the lucky ones did, a lot of juicy orders. That is free enterprise and how it

149

differs from feudalism or mercantilism or socialism or Bolshevism.

If it had all meant something, the meaning would have been vitiated by Henry Luce's closing speech. Here was a man with the finest speech-writing talent in the world at his disposal, but this one he unquestionably insisted on writing himself. There were rumors all over the place that *Time-Life* was going to announce a new international business magazine and that this was all an elaborate promotion scheme. Expensive, but paid off by three or four full page ads. That would have been bad taste enough, but the Luce denouement was simply pathetic. After all the high-flown internationalism, it was intensely local, directed at the American Republicans present exclusively. It was the baldest appeal for the election of Richard Nixon to the Presidency and, in the meantime, a high, preferably a cabinet, post for Mr. Luce. It was like some awful little girl reciting "The Dream of Eugene Aram" for company. Everybody was so embarrassed. And it contained the rhetorical masterpiece of the year: "And I have no doubt that the words spoken here, the informal words equally as important as the formal, *are already circling the heart waves of mankind*, inviting thousands of men and women of energy and faith to be of our number in the conquest of the future in Freedom's name." Italics, like they say, are mine. Sort of a scientific breakthrough, the combination of the wave and corpuscle theory of heartbeats. Oh, Mr. Luce, I want to like you, I think you do a lot of good with things like the Faubus cover story and all, but how could you?

150

As an impartial observer, what are the conclusions to be drawn? The so-called Free World divides pretty clearly into three groups. The USA, Canada, and Australia, the other predominantly white or white-governed Dominions, Latin America, to a much lesser degree, Great Britain itself —these comprise the first group. The industrialists and financiers of this group are optimistic about the future of "free enterprise." They believe in it as a gospel, and they see no reason why it can't solve the world's economic problems if given a chance in a friendly environment. They look on all state interference as "creeping Bolshevism" and on the kind of racial and national awakening shown at Bandung as dangerous demagogy. They are not inspired by malice, they are perfectly confident they can help. In fact, especially in the lower echelons of the American business community, there is enormous good will. Typical go-getters, these minor businessmen are friendly as six-month pups. What is wrong is simply ethnocentrism. The economic and social problems of, say, Indonesia, are more incomprehensible to them than the outlandish religious practices of Bali. This is the greatest and last of all social blockages. After all the American Indian and the white man have stood irreconcilably distinct for 500 years, in spite of every kind of good and bad will on both sides.

Second are the Continental Europeans, but especially the West Germans and French. (The French didn't even bother to send anyone important, apparently on the principle of "give a _____ an inch and he'll take a yard.") They are for strong measures. Not because they have confidence in capitalism, but because they don't. The motto used to be "it will last our time." Now it seems to be "it will last till I can get it converted into gold and get it in a bank vault in Montevideo." The Americans, unfortunately, are committed to this world, as well as to the world of Bandung.

Last, the "native" capitalists. As I have said, they are incomparably better educated, more aware of what is going on, than are their Western colleagues. They know that the economic development of the Asian and African peoples must rely on a large percentage of socialism, or at least state sponsored, financed, and guided capital investment. And, of course, the foreign investment too must be largely state originated. We forget that Point Four or the Marshall Plan is "socialist" in the invidious sense. There simply isn't enough private capital available. They want to help, and they want to preserve their social advantages in their own country. After all, they are members of a tiny élite in a mass of poverty and illiteracy. So tiny in fact, that as anyone who knows, for instance, India, is aware, it's like Holland or Denmark—"everybody knows everybody else" —steel barons, members of Parliament, Surrealists, Trotskyites, physicists, newspapermen, movie actresses, bankers. On this élite depends the future of the country. And the first loyalty of the Asian capitalist is, in almost every case, to this caste and to his people as a whole, and not to the international business community, and least of all to an abstraction like Free Enterprise.

Until the American government and the American businessman understand this, nothing is going to happen but frustration. And the more the frustration increases, the further, of course, the already wide gulf between the two is going to spread. The best thing about the whole conference is that it did show, if you wanted to ferret it out, a real effort to understand on the part of many American businessmen, who were, unfortunately neither in the majority nor in, usually, determinative positions. But there was certainly plenty of good will. If the accelerating avalanches of economic and social difficulty don't overwhelm this good will, it may, eventually, be enough—not to prevent socialism, but to ameliorate catastrophe.

# THE REALITY OF
# HENRY MILLER

It is a wonderful thing that some of Henry Miller's work at last is coming out in a popular edition in the United States. Henry Miller is a really popular writer, a writer of and for real people, who, in other countries, is read, not just by highbrows, or just by the wider public which reads novels, but by common people, by the people who, in the United States, read comic books. As the Southern mountain woman said of her hero son, dead in Korea, "Mister, he was sure a great reader, always settin' in the corner with a piece of cold bread and one of them funny books." In Czech and Japanese, this is the bulk of Miller's public. In the United States he has been kept away from a popular public and his great novels have been banned; therefore only highbrows who could import them from France have read him.

I once crossed the Atlantic—eighteen days in a Compagnie Générale Transatlantique freighter—with a cabin mate, a French African Negro, who was only partially literate, but who was able to talk for hours on the comparative merits of *Black Spring* and the *Tropic of Cancer* and the *Tropic of Capricorn*. When he found out I came from California and knew Miller, he started treating me as if I were an archangel newly descended, and never tired of questions about *le Beeg Sur* and *les camarades de M'sieu Millaire*. He had a mental picture of poor Henry living on a mountain-top, surrounded by devoted handmaids and a bevy of zoot-suited existentialist jitterbugs.

This picture, I have discovered, is quite commonly believed in by people who should have better sense. Miners in the Pyrenees, camel drivers in Tlemcen, gondoliers in Venice, and certainly every *poule* in Paris, when they hear you're from California, ask, first thing, in one voice, "Do you know *M'sieu Millaire?*" This doesn't mean he isn't read by the intellectuals, the cultured people over there. He is. In fact, I should say he has become part of the standard repertory of reading matter everywhere but in England and the United States. If you have read Balzac, or Baudelaire, or Goethe, you are also expected to have read Miller. He is certainly one of the most widely read American writers, along with Upton Sinclair, Jack London, Fenimore Cooper, William Faulkner and Erskine Caldwell.

This is the way it should be. Nothing was sadder than the "proletarian novelist" of a few years back, the product of a sociology course and a subscription to a butcher-paper weekly, eked out with a terrified visit to a beer parlor on the other side of the tracks and a hasty scurry past a picket line. Nobody read him but other Greenwich Village aesthetes like himself. The people Henry Miller writes about read him. They read him because he gives them something they cannot find elsewhere in print. It may not be precisely the real world, but it is nearer to it than most other writing, and it is certainly nearer than most so-called realistic writing.

Once the written work was the privilege of priests and

155

priestly scribes. Although thousands of years have passed,
vestiges of that special privilege and caste artificiality still
cling to it. It has been said that literature is a class phenomenon. Can you remember when you first started to
read? Doubtless you thought that some day you would find
in books the truth, the answer to the very puzzling life you
were discovering around you. But you never did. If you
were alert, you discovered that books were conventions, as
unlike life as a game of chess. The written word is a sieve.
Only so much of reality gets through as fits the size and
shape of the screen, and in some ways that is never enough.
This is only partly due to the necessary conventions of
speech, writing, communication generally. Partly it is due
to the structure of language. With us, in our Western European civilization, this takes the form of Indo-European
grammar crystallized in what we call Aristotelian logic.
But most of the real difficulty of communication comes
from social convention, from a vast conspiracy to agree to
accept the world as something it really isn't at all. Even the
realistic novels of a writer like Zola are not much closer to
the real thing than the documents written in Egyptian
hieroglyphics. They are just a different, most complex distortion.

Literature is a social defense mechanism. Remember
again when you were a child. You thought that some day
you would grow up and find a world of real adults—the
people who really made things run—and understood how
and why things ran. People like the Martian aristocrats in
science fiction. Your father and mother were pretty silly,

and the other grownups were even worse—but somewhere, some day, you'd find the real grownups and possibly even be admitted to their ranks. Then, as the years went on, you learned, through more or less bitter experience, that there aren't, and never have been, any such people, anywhere. Life is just a mess, full of tall children, grown stupider, less alert and resilient, and nobody knows what makes it go —as a whole, or any part of it. *But nobody ever tells.*

Henry Miller tells. Anderson told *about* the little boy and the Emperor's new clothes. Miller is the little boy himself. He tells about the Emperor, about the pimples on his behind, and the warts on his private parts, and the dirt between his toes. Other writers in the past have done this, of course, and they are the great ones, the real classics. But they have done it within the conventions of literature. They have used the forms of the Great Lie to expose the truth. Some of this literature is comic, with a terrifying laughter —Cervantes' *Don Quixote*, Jonson's *Volpone*, Machiavelli's *Mandragola*, Shakespeare's *King Lear*. Some of it is tragic, in the ordinary sense, like the *Iliad*, or Thucydides' history, or *Macbeth*. In the last analysis it is all tragic, even Rabelais, because life itself is tragic. With very few exceptions, however, it is all conventional. It disguises itself in the garments of harmless artistic literature. It sneaks in and betrays the complacent and deluded. A great work of art is a kind of Trojan Horse. There are those who believe that this is all there is to the art of poetry—sugar-coating the pills of prussic acid with which the poet doses the Enemy.

It is hard to tell sometimes when Miller is being ironic

and when he is being naïve. He is the master of a deadpan
style, just as he has a public personality that alternates between quiet gentleness—"like a dentist," he describes it—
and a sort of deadpan buffoonery. This has led some critics
to consider him a naïve writer, a "modern primitive," like
the painter Rousseau. In a sense this is true.

Miller is a very unliterary writer. He writes as if he had
just invented the alphabet. When he writes about a book,
he writes as if he were the first and only man who had ever
read it—and, furthermore, as if it weren't a book but a
piece of the living meat whacked off Balzac or Rimbaud or
whoever. Rousseau was one of the finest painters of modern
times. But he was absolutely impervious to the ordinary devices of his craft. This was not because he was not exposed
to other artists. He spent hours every week in the Louvre,
and he was, from the 1880s to the eve of the First World
War, the intimate of all the best painters and writers, the
leading intellectuals of Paris. It didn't make any difference. He just went his way, being Henri Rousseau, a very
great artist. But when he talked or wrote, he spouted terrible nonsense. He wasn't just a crank, but quite off his
rocker in an amiable sort of way. This is not true of Miller.

In some mysterious way, Miller has preserved an innocence of the practice of Literature-with-a-capital-L which is
almost unique in history. Likewise he has preserved an innocence of heart. But he is not unsophisticated. In the first
place, he writes a muscular, active prose in which something is always going on and which is always under control.
True, he often rambles and gets windy, but only because he

likes to ramble and hear his head roar. When he wants to tell you something straight from the shoulder, he makes you reel.

Now the writer most like Miller in some ways, the eighteenth-century naïf, Restif de la Bretonne, is certainly direct from the innocent heart, but he can be as tedious as a year's mail of a Lonely Hearts Club, with the same terrible verisimilitude of a "Mature woman, broadminded, likes books and music" writing to "Bachelor, fifty-two, steady job, interested in finer things." And, in addition, Restif is full of arrant nonsense, every variety of crackpot notion. If you want the common man of the eighteenth century, with his heart laid bare, you will find him in Restif. But you will also find thousands of pages of sheer boredom, and hundreds of pages of quite loony and obviously invented pornography. Miller too is likely at times to go off the deep end about the lost continent of Mu or astrology or the "occult," but it is for a different reason. If the whole shebang is a lie anyway, certainly the amusing lies, the lies of the charlatans who have never been able to get the guillotine in their hands, are better than the official lie, the deadly one. Since Hiroshima, this attitude needs little apology. Some of our best people prefer alchemy to physics today.

There aren't many people like Miller in all literature. The only ones I can think of are Petronius, Casanova, and Restif. They all tried to be absolutely honest. Their books give an overwhelming feeling of being true, the real thing, completely uncooked. They are all intensely masculine writers. They are all great comic writers. They all convey, in every case very powerfully, a constant sense of the utter tragedy of life. I can think of no more chilling, scalp-raising passages in literature than the tolling of the bell from the very beginning of Casanova's *Memoirs:* the comments and asides of the aged man writing of his splendid youth, an old, sick, friendless pauper in a drafty castle in the backwoods of Bohemia. And last, and most important, they were all what the English call "spivs." Courtier of Nero or Parisian typesetter, they were absolutely uninvolved; they just didn't give a damn whether school kept or not.

The French like to compare Miller with Sade. But nowadays they like to compare everybody with Sade. It is the currently fashionable form of Babbitt-baiting over there. The comparison is frivolous. Sade is unbelievably tedious; Diderot stood on his head, a bigot without power, an unemployed Robespierre. In the eighteenth century the French writers most like Miller are the "primitive" Restif, and Mirabeau when, in some of his personal writings, he really works up a lather.

Miller has often been compared with Céline, but I don't think the comparison is apposite. Céline is a man with a thesis; furthermore, he is a litterateur. In *Journey to the End of the Night*, he set out to write the epic of a Robinson Crusoe of the modern soul, the utterly alienated man. He did it, very successfully. Céline and his friends stumble through the fog, over the muddy ruts with the body of Robinson, in a denouement as monumental as the *Nibelungenlied*. But it is all a work of art. I have been in the neighborhoods Céline describes. They simply aren't that awful. I am sure, on internal evidence of the story itself, that his family wasn't that bad. And, like Malraux and some others, he is obsessed with certain marginal sexual activities which he drags in all the time, willy-nilly.

Céline makes a sociological judgment on Robinson. Miller is Robinson, and, on the whole, he finds it a bearable role, even enjoyable in its way. The modern French writers who most resemble Miller are Carco, without the formulas, Mac Orlan, if he weren't so slick, Artaud, if he weren't crazy, and Blaise Cendrars. Cendrars is a good European and Miller is only an amateur European, but Europe has been going on so long that the insights of the amateur are often much more enlightening.

Henry Miller is often spoken of as a religious writer. To some this just seems silly, because Miller is not especially profound. People expect religion to come to them vested in miracle, mystery, and authority, as Dostoevski said. The founders of the major religions are pretty well hidden from us by the accumulation of centuries of interpretation, the dirt of history—the lie you prefer to believe. Perhaps originally they weren't so mysterious and miraculous and authoritarian. Mohammed lived in the light of history. We can form a pretty close idea of what he was like, and he wasn't very prepossessing in some ways. He was just naïvely direct. With the simple-mindedness of a camel driver he cut through the welter of metaphysics and mystification in the Near East of his time. Blake dressed his message up in sonorous and mysterious language; but the message itself is simple enough. D. H. Lawrence likewise. You could write it all on a postage stamp: "Mene, mene, tekel, upharsin. Your official reality is a lie. We must love one another or die." I suppose any writer who transcends conventional literature is religious insofar as he does transcend it. That is why you can never actually base an educational system on the "Hundred Best Books." A hundred of the truest insights into life as it is would destroy any educational system and its society along with it.

Certainly Miller is almost completely untouched by what is called religion in England and America and northern Europe. He is completely pagan. This is why his book on Greece, *The Colossus of Maroussi,* is a book of self-discovery as well as a very true interpretation of Greece. It is thoroughly classic. Although he never mentions Homer and dismisses the Parthenon, he did discover the life of Greece: the common, real life of peasants and fishermen, going on, just as it has gone on ever since the Doric invasions. A world of uncompromised people, of people if not like Miller himself, at least like the man he knew he wanted to be.

His absolute freedom from the Christian or Jewish anguish of conscience, the sense of guilt, implication, and compromise, makes Miller humane, maybe even humanistic, but it effectively keeps him from being humanitarian. He might cry over a pet dog who had been run over, or even punch the guilty driver in the nose. He might have assassinated Hitler if he had had the chance. He would never join the Society for the Prevention of Cruelty to

Animals or the Friends' Service Committee. He is not involved in the guilt, and so in no way is he involved in the penance. This comes out in everything he writes, and it offends lots of people. Others may go to bullfights and write novels preaching the brotherhood of man. Miller just doesn't go to the bullfight in the first place. So, although he often raves, he never preaches. People have been taught to expect preaching, practically unadulterated, in even the slick fiction of the women's magazines, and they are offended now if they don't find it.

Fifty per cent of the people in this country don't vote. They simply don't want to be implicated in organized society. With, in most cases, a kind of animal instinct, they know that they cannot really do anything about it, that the participation offered them is a hoax. And even if it weren't, they know that if they don't participate, they aren't implicated, at least not voluntarily. It is for these people, the submerged fifty per cent, that Miller speaks. As the newspapers never tire of pointing out, this is a very American attitude. Miller says, "I am a patriot—of the Fourteenth Ward of Brooklyn, where I was raised." For him life has never lost that simplicity and immediacy. Politics is the deal in the saloon back room. Law is the cop on the beat, shaking down whores and helping himself to apples. Religion is Father Maguire and Rabbi Goldstein, and their actual congregations. Civilization is the Telegraph Company in *Tropic of Capricorn*. All this is a quite different story to the art critics and the literary critics and those strange people the newspapers call "pundits" and "solons."

163

I am sure the editors of our butcher-paper liberal magazines have never sat in the back room of a sawdust saloon and listened to the politicians divide up the take from the brothels that line the boundary streets of their wards. If they did, they would be outraged and want to bring pressure to bear in the State Capitol. With Miller, that is just the way things are, and what of it?

So there isn't any social message in Miller, except an absolute one. When you get through reading the realistic novels of James Farrell or Nelson Algren, you have a nasty suspicion that the message of the author is: "More playgrounds and properly guided social activities will reduce crime and vice." There is nothing especially frightful about Miller's Brooklyn; like Farrell's South Side, it is just life in the lower middle class and upper working class section of a big American city. It certainly isn't what queasy reviewers call it, "the slums." It's just the life the reviewers themselves led before they became reviewers. What outrages them is that Miller accepts it, just as do the people who still live there. Accepting it, how he can write about it? He can bring back the whole pre-World War I America— the bunny hug, tunes from *The Pink Lady*, Battling Nelson, Dempsey the Nonpareil, Pop Anson and Pearl White, a little boy rushing the growler with a bucket of suds and a sack of six-inch pretzels in the smoky twilight of a Brooklyn Sunday evening.

I think that is what Miller found in Paris. Not the city of Art, Letters, and Fashion—but prewar Brooklyn. It is certainly what I like best about Paris, and it is what I get out

of Miller's writing about Paris. He is best about Paris
where it is still most like 1910 Brooklyn. He doesn't write
about the Latin Quarter, but about the dim-lit streets and
dusty little squares which lie between the Latin Quarter and
the Jardin des Plantes, where men sit drinking beer in their
shirt sleeves in front of dirty little bars in another smoky
Sunday twilight. He is better about the jumble of streets
between Montrouge and Montparnasse with its polyglot and
polychrome population of the very poor, than he is about
Montparnasse itself and its artists' life. He practically ignores Montmartre; apparently he concludes that only suck-
ers go there. But he writes very convincingly about that most
Brooklyn-like of all the quarters of Paris, the district near
the Military Academy on the Place du Champs de Mars,
now filling up with Algerians and Negroes, where the subway becomes an elevated, tall tenements mingle with small
bankrupt factories and people sit on the doorsteps fanning
themselves in the Brooklyn-like summer heat, and sleep
and couple on the summer roofs.

So his intellectuals in Paris are assimilated to Brooklyn.
They may talk about Nietzsche and Dostoevski, but they
talk like hall-room boys, rooming together, working at odd
jobs, picking up girls in dance halls and parks. "Batching"
is the word. Over the most impassioned arguments and the
bawdiest conversations lingers an odor of unwashed socks.
The light is the light of Welsbach mantles on detachable
cuffs and unmade beds. Of course that is the way they
really talked, still do for that matter.

There is a rank, old-fashioned masculinity about this

165

world which shocks the tender-minded and self-deluded. It is far removed from the Momism of the contemporary young American male. This is why Miller is accused of writing about all women as though they were whores, never treating them as "real persons," as equals. This is why he is said to lack any sense of familial love. On the whole, I think this is true. Most of the sexual encounters in the *Tropics* and *The Rosy Crucifixion* are comic accidents, as impersonal as a pratfall. The woman never emerges at all. He characteristically writes of his wives as bad boys talk of their schoolteachers. When he takes his sexual relations seriously, the woman disappears in a sort of marshy cyclone. She becomes an erotic giantess, a perambulating orgy. Although Miller writes a lot about his kinship with D. H. Lawrence, he has very little of Lawrence's abiding sense of the erotic couple, of man and woman as the two equal parts of a polarity which takes up all of life. This again is Brooklyn, pre-suffragette Brooklyn. And I must admit that it is true, at least for almost everybody. A real wedding of equals, a truly sacramental marriage in which every bit of both personalities, and all the world with them, is transmuted and glorified, may exist; in fact, some people may have a sort of talent for it; but it certainly isn't very common. And the Great Lie, the social hoax in which we live, has taken the vision of this transcendent state and turned it into its cheapest hoax and its most powerful lie. I don't see why Miller should be blamed if he has never found it. Hardly anybody ever does, and those who do usually lose it in some sordid fashion. This, of course, is

166

the point, the message, if you want a message, of all his encounters in parks and telephone booths and brothels. Better this than the lie. Better the flesh than the World and the Devil. And this is why these passages are not pornographic, but comic like *King Lear* and tragic like *Don Quixote*.

At least once, Miller makes up for this lack. The tale of the *Cosmodemonic Telegraph Company* in *Tropic of Capricorn* is a perfect portrait of our insane and evil society. It says the same thing others have said, writing on primitive accumulation or on the condition of the working class, and it says it far more convincingly. This is human self-alienation at its uttermost, and not just theoretically, or even realistically. It is an orgy of human self-alienation, a cesspool of it, and Miller rubs your nose in it. Unless you are a prig and a rascal, when you get through, you know, once and for all, what is the matter. And through it all, like Beatrice, if Beatrice had guided Dante through the Inferno, moves the figure of Valeska, who had Negro blood and who kills herself at the end—one of the most real women in fiction, if you want to call it fiction.

Once Miller used to have pinned on his bedroom door a scrap of paper. Written on it was "S'agapo"—the Greek for "I love you." In *The Alcoholic Veteran* he says, "The human heart cannot be broken."

# MARK TOBEY:
# PAINTER OF THE
# HUMANE ABSTRACT

Through the month of April and the first week of May [1951], the California Palace of the Legion of Honor is showing a comprehensive exhibit of the work of Mark Tobey. It is a very large show, one of the largest I have ever seen devoted to a contemporary American painter. With a small background exhibit of Chinese calligraphy, it fills just half the museum. This is a lot of painting, and it makes it possible to come to some fairly definite conclusions about Tobey, his influence, his development, his significance.

As I left the show, I came on a little case with a tatter of ancient Peruvian cloth, two tones of dim, worn red crossed with angular lines of white. For hundreds of years it had lain close to the body of a Peruvian woman while the processes of final mortality seeped through it. It seemed to be saturated with the pathetic fallacy of life itself. The white threads meandered like withering thoughts over once fleshy reds now almost grey. From a little distance it looked so exactly like a Tobey that I thought some of the show had overflowed into an outer corridor.

There are many objects like that in Tobey's studio. Certain painters, writers, philosophers, a religious temper of

168

life, other big things, have given his art its form and inner meaning. Objects, artifacts, like this one, have given it its tone and superficial appearances. His later pictures "look like" things made with a draftsman's sensuality, but worn and broken, the colors all faded to white or dulled to grey except the blurred mineral reds.

Of important artists today Tobey is one of the most completely self-educated. For this reason he is independently, widely, and seriously educated, at home in those provinces of art and thought, distant in time or space, which interest him. He has assimilated only what he wanted, but he has wanted much, and he has been thorough about it. His influences may, until recently, lie off the mainstreams of modern artistic ancestry, but they are completely part of him.

Tobey was born in Centerville, Wisconsin, December 11, 1890. At twenty he went to New York and had his first exhibitions, at Knoedler's and Romany Marie's, of portrait drawings. For a few years he alternated between New York and Chicago. Then he went out to Seattle to teach at the Cornish School. In those days Seattle was still in the flush of a regional awakening which was sparked by the intellectuals around the I.W.W. Figures like Jimmy Chaplin, Charley Ashleigh, Ted Abrams, Morris Pass, flamboyant characters from the last frontiers who read Ernest Dowson and Carl Sandburg, admired Beardsley and Van Gogh, rode boxcars, soapboxed, got shot at and put in jail, were the leaders of a bohemian radicalism that was certainly closer to actual "workers on the march" than the proletarian aesthetes of the depression period. The Wobbly

Preamble, Free Verse, The New Art, Free Love, and lots of straight whiskey . . . they were not enough to found the new society which then seemed just around the corner, but they were plenty for a short-lived, boisterous renaissance. Those years were formative. I met Tobey then in Seattle. He was painting skidrow figures, migratory workers, lumberjacks, and sailors. They were not very good pictures. Twenty-five years later, he is still painting the same kind of models. They are very good pictures. I don't want to suggest that he is a proletarian artist. He is about as far from it as possible. But his art is not just abstract, "forms and dispositions of places and positions," as Gertrude Stein said of Cubism. It is also humane. It started being that way, however clumsily, at the beginning.

In 1925–26, Tobey traveled in Europe and the Near East. In those days he must have started looking long and hard at paintings whose influence was to show up many years later. In 1927 he returned to Seattle. From 1931 to 1938 he taught at Dartington Hall, Totnes, Devon, England, and traveled extensively in Europe, Mexico, and the Far East. In 1934 he was in China and Japan. He became deeply interested in Chinese calligraphy, and his present style began to take form. Since 1938 he has been back in Seattle.

The earliest Tobeys are not in this show. It starts with some simple landscapes and still lives, and other exercises, of value chiefly for showing how little the young Tobey was touched by the sophisticated taste of that time. They are careful, honest, and clumsy. Then come some typical early

American abstractions, like 1920 Chicago, or the post-Armory explosion of half a generation earlier. They are notable for their modest color in a day when, in America, "modernism" meant "loud." Considerably later come some studies of wave motion. Space is considered as being defined by moving forces rather than occupied by volumes. The impact of the picture is carefully muted; range of color, value, hue, all the elements are reduced and quieted. There is just the beginning in the smoky reds of *Modal Tides* of the influence of Tintoretto. This was the right track, if only the beginning. There would be divagations and side experiments, but the field of a very special sensibility had been found.

Sometimes in those years of travel Tobey must have stood a long time in the Doge's Palace and the Scuola San Rocco, looking finally and longest at things many people do not consider important—the interplay of gauzy drapery, blades of low lit grass, rippling water and light—the cob-webbed space in the Annunciation—the black and white chinoiseries of the other St. Marys—the batlike silhouettes (due to faulty retouching) which plunge through the Paradiso; and even at paintings which most people consider dull—the studio jobs of battle scenes, mostly the work of Aliense, that well-named man, and the younger Robusti—vast dull red paintings, filled with rigging and spars, hedges and waves of spears, beams and bars of dark and light, fire and smoke, and, lacing all the spaces, serried flights of arrows. He must have absorbed, too, some of the peculiar space of Tintoretto, which, though not rushing

171

infinitely up and away like the ceilings of later Counter-Reformation Baroque, seems to have no limits, no bottom or top or end—only an inexhaustible ruddy vastness. There are other Venetian echoes—the desolate, simple faces of Longhi, the splashing brush work of Guardi, even Tiepolo could have contributed something, the calligraphic Tiepolo of the half transformed *Actaeon* and the other black background pictures in the corridor of the Academia.

After the studies of wave motion come some texture paintings, then some stiffly-placed still lives in tones of grey, and some dark, transparent Cubist ones, rather like Tamayo or Gris, essentially volumes in space—accomplished, but not Tobey's metier, and then back to filled space. At first the space is filled with tumbling volumes, for instance in *Pinnacles,* which gives something of the impression of a Pontormo drawing, or of Tobey's colleague, Kenneth Callahan, and finally the emergence of a fully calligraphic style.

The first calligraphic pictures are organized along poles in three dimensions, usually swaths of bright color, the calligraphy widely spaced, sparkling black or very dark lines, sometimes outlined with a glow, on white or neutral backgrounds. This is abandoned, probably as too confined, still too close to the painting of objects. The backgrounds get dimmer and smokier and their almost invisible modulations create shifting depths which are only variations of indefinitely expanding monochrome.

With *Broadway Norm* in 1935, the lines become predominantly white; the "white writing" now identified with

Tobey has appeared. The darker lines and the background create a movement in deep space which is caught and defined and, as the eye travels, continuously molded by the overlapping nets of pale grey and white. The first of its kind, *Broadway Norm* is formally a rather simple picture, small, a first step.

This major change follows the year spent in the Far East. Is this new turn Chinese in any very complete sense? I think not. I have a feeling that the great art of China is too much for Tobey. It was a determinative influence in the change itself, the deliberate adoption of calligraphy, but the Sung landscapists and their Zenist descendants in Japan are a great deal more than calligraphers. I am afraid their scope, and the capacity and conditions for their inexhaustible peace—an ontological peace—are gone from the world. For all Tobey's openness to Oriental influence, he is still another Western Man, like the rest of us, troubled and doomed. His ancestors are in Venice, the West's window on the Orient in the crucial centuries, and his cousins are the later Turner and Odilon Redon. Seattle today, of course, like San Francisco, has a commercial position analogous to Renaissance Venice, and its Museum contains some of the better works of the former Eumorfopoulos Collection of Far Eastern art. I suspect that Tobey, who was in England at the time of the sale, may have had something to do with this purchase.

This brings up another influence which must be mentioned. Before the Eumorfopoulos purchase there wasn't very much art in Seattle of any importance, except the work

173

of the Northwest Indians. Tobey has spent much time in Indian villages, owns several fine examples of their work, has purchased much for others, and has steered his students toward careful study of Northwest Indian motives and methods. Some of his paintings, notably *Eskimo Idiom* in this show, use these motives directly. In this instance the forms of masks, ivory carvings, and implements are built up as on a shield. The first impression is rather like that of analytical Cubism. Then a sense of transparency and interpenetration comes as a sharp surprise after the picture has been seen for a while, and at last the forms resolve themselves into calligraphic vectors, directions of tensions. In other pictures the idiom of Northwest woodcarving and textiles is immediately resolved into pure calligraphy. Incidentally, it should not be forgotten that this idiom is so close to that of primitive Japan, Ainu, and Shang bronze that critics like Fenollosa have postulated the existence of a Pacific Basin primitive formal endowment, a plastic "culture complex" as pervasive as that of La Tene in Europe.

I think, actually, this Northwest idiom shows most strongly in a group of massed figure paintings, of which *The Gathering* (1944) is a good example. The faces have the same mask-like quality, the bodies the same tense stiffness, wooden but dynamic. But there are other aspects too, ultimately more important. The overall color is one of dirty flesh, as crowded as Rowlandson, and again, like him, calligraphic, but in Tobey's case not the War of the Fat and the Lean, but a more fundamental conflict. Possibly this particular painting is an artists' ball. The effect is that of a skidrow mission on Christmas Eve, crowded with ungainly movement, busy with aimlessness and embarrassment. Here and there expectant, bemused faces stare into the air above the spectator's head, so that he feels "overlooked" with incomprehension—unemployed shepherds watching the caroling angels as cripples watch skywriters. It makes no difference, artists' ball or hoboes' feast, the judgment is the same.

In two slightly variant paintings, *Skidrow Figures* (1948), studies in isolated silhouette, rather like Morris Graves, this judgment is intensified. The figures slip away from human into reptilian or birdlike forms. One central one rises into a kind of supplication, a Gethsemane of the gutter.

Similar in tone are the paintings of city streets, *Flow of the Night, Broadway,* many others, saturated complexes of calligraphic light filled with little people. An electron model spins; lines of women move away on an escalator; an aged whore stands like a verger at the door of an English cathedral; a desolate flophouse room, inhabited by a sinister little vortex, floats in space; ears bloom in the air; a nude is hung up by the heels; and everywhere, men with the wise, battered, hopeless faces of aging migratory workers wander, eyes lost in space, not even bothering to ogle the girls' legs.

Finally come the pure calligraphic abstractions, *Chrysalis, City Radiance,* a whole series of paintings which are the culmination to date of Tobey's art. *City Radiance* is a complete crystallization of space, straight lines meet-

175

ing mostly in acute angles and equilaterals, with rectangles traveling across like sonorous pedal notes, the whole volume doubly folded, envelope-wise, on itself and, across the fold, a form, defined by rising lines, somewhat like Brancusi's birds, and like them, ineffably soaring. These pictures are the other side of the coin, the religious affirmation which supersedes the mordant analysis of the mind of benighted cities. After all, the title is *City Radiance*. The pictures of this group may be abstract, but their calm and order and purity grow technically and personally, and even representationally in a sense, out of knowledge of suffering and disorder and brutal ignorance. This is compassion. In these paintings Tobey touches the tradition of the Zen landscapists. He is a humane painter.

# POETRY,
# REGENERATION,
# AND D. H. LAWRENCE

At the very beginning Lawrence belonged to a different order of being from the literary writers of his day. In 1912 he said: "I worship Christ, I worship Jehovah, I worship Pan, I worship Aphrodite. But I do not worship hands nailed and running with blood upon a cross, nor licentiousness, nor lust. I want them all, all the gods. They are all God. But I must serve in real love. If I take my whole passionate, spiritual and physical love to the woman who in turn loves me, that is how I serve God. And my hymn and my game of joy is my work. All of which I read in . . ."

Do you know what he read all that in? It makes you wince. He thought he found that in *Georgian Poetry, 1911–1912!* In Lascelles Abercrombie, Wilfred Gibson, John Drinkwater, Rupert Brooke, John Masefield, Walter de la Mare, Gordon Bottomley! What a good man Lawrence must have been. It is easy to understand how painful it was for him to learn what evil really was. It is easy to understand why the learning killed him, slowly and terribly. But he never gave up. He was always hunting for comradeship— in the most unlikely places—Michael Arlen, Peter Warlock, Murry, Mabel Dodge. He never stopped trusting

177

people and hoping. And he went on writing exactly the gospel he announced in 1912, right to the end.

Lawrence thought he was a Georgian, at first. There are people who will tell you that his early poetry was typical Georgian countryside poetry—*Musings in the Hedgerows,* by the Well Dressed Dormouse. It is true that early poems like "The Wild Common," "Cherry Robbers," and the others, bear a certain resemblance to the best Georgian verse. They are rhymed verse in the English language on "subjects taken from nature." Some of the Georgians had a favorite literary convention. They were anti-literary. Lawrence was the real thing. His "hard" rhymes, for instance, "quick-kick," "rushes-pushes," "sheepdip-soft lip," "gudgeon-run on." I don't imagine that when Lawrence came to "soft lip" he remembered that bees had always sipped at soft lips and that, as a representative of a new tendency, it was up to him to do something about it. I think his mind just moved in regions not covered by the standard associations of standard British rhyme patterns. At the end of his life he was still talking about the old sheep dip, with its steep soft lip of turf, in the village where he was born. Why, once he even rhymed "wind" and "thinned," in the most unaware manner imaginable. That is something that, to the best of my knowledge, has never been done before or since in the British Isles.

The hard metric, contorted and distorted and generally banged around, doesn't sound made up, either. Compulsion neurotics like Hopkins and querulous old gentlemen like Bridges made quite an art of metrical eccentricity. You turned an iamb into a trochee here, and an anapest into a hard spondee there, and pretty soon you got something that sounded difficult and tortured and intense. I think Lawrence was simply very sensitive to quantity and to the cadenced pulses of verse. In the back of his head was a stock of sundry standard English verse patterns. He started humming a poem, hu hu hum, hum hum, hu hu hum hu, adjusted it as best might be to the remembered accentual patterns, and let it go at that. I don't think he was unconscious of the new qualities which emerged, but I don't think he went about it deliberately, either.

This verse is supposed to be like Hardy's. It is. But there is always something a little synthetic about Hardy's rugged verse. The smooth ones seem more natural, somehow. The full dress, Matthew Arnold sort of sonnet to Leslie Stephen is probably Hardy's best poem. It is a very great poem, but Arnold learned the trick of talking like a highly idealized Anglican archbishop and passed it on to Hardy. That is something nobody could imagine Lawrence ever learning; he just wasn't that kind of an animal.

Hardy could say to himself: "Today I am going to be a Wiltshire yeoman, sitting on a fallen rock at Stonehenge, writing a poem to my girl on a piece of wrapping paper with the gnawed stub of a pencil," and he could make it very convincing. But Lawrence really was the educated son of a coal miner, sitting under a tree that had once been part of Sherwood Forest, in a village that was rapidly becoming part of a world-wide, disemboweled hell, writing hard, painful poems, to girls who carefully had been taught

179

the art of unlove. It was all real. Love really was a mystery at the navel of the earth, like Stonehenge. The miner really was in contact with a monstrous, seething mystery, the black sun in the earth. There is a vatic quality in Lawrence that is only in Hardy rarely, in a few poems, and in great myths like *Two on a Tower*.

Something breaks out of the Pre-Raphaelite landscape of "Cherry Robbers." That poem isn't like a Victorian imitation of medieval illumination at all. It is more like one of those crude Coptic illuminations, with the Christian content just a faint glaze over the black, bloody "Babylonian turbulence" of the Gnostic mystery. I don't know the date of the "Hymn to Priapus," it seems to lie somewhere between his mother's death and his flight with Frieda, but it is one of the Hardy kind of poems, and it is one of Lawrence's best. It resembles Hardy's "Night of the Dance." But there is a difference. Hardy is so anxious to be common that he just avoids being commonplace. Lawrence *is* common, he doesn't have to try. He is coming home from a party, through the winter fields, thinking of his dead mother, of the girl he has just had in the barn, of his troubled love life, and suddenly Orion leans down out of the black heaven and touches him on the thigh, and the hair of his head stands up.

Hardy was a major poet. Lawrence was a minor prophet. Like Blake and Yeats, his is the greater tradition. If Hardy ever had a girl in the hay, tipsy on cider, on the night of Boxing Day, he kept quiet about it. He may have thought that it had something to do with "the stream of his life in the darkness deathward set," but he never let on, except indirectly.

Good as they are, there is an incompleteness about the early poems. They are the best poetry written in England at that time, but they are poems of hunger and frustration. Lawrence was looking for completion. He found it later, of course, in Frieda, but he hadn't found it then. The girl he called Miriam wrote a decent, conscientious contribution to his biography. She makes it only too obvious that what he was looking for was not to be found in her. And so the Miriam poems are tortured, and defeated, and lost, as though Lawrence didn't know where he was, which was literally true.

Between Miriam and Frieda lies a body of even more intense and troubled poems. Those to his mother, the dialect poems, and the poems to Helen are in this group. The "mother" poems are among his best. They are invaluable as direct perspectives on an extraordinary experience.

From one point of view Lawrence is the last of a special tradition that begins with St. Augustine and passes through Pascal and Baudelaire amongst others, to end finally in himself. There is no convincing evidence for Freud's theory that the Oedipus Complex dates back to some extremely ancient crime in the history of primitive man. Least of all is there any Oedipus Complex in the Oedipus myth or plays. There is ample evidence that Western European civilization is specifically the culture of the Oedipus Complex. Before Augustine there was nothing really like it. There were fore-runners and prototypes and intimations, but there wasn't

181

the real thing. The *Confessions* introduce a new sickness of the human mind, the most horrible pandemic, and the most lethal, ever to afflict man. Augustine did what silly literary boys in our day boast of doing. He invented a new derangement. If you make an intense effort to clear your mind and then read Baudelaire and Catullus together, the contrast, the new thing in Baudelaire, makes you shudder. Baudelaire is struggling in a losing battle with a ghost more powerful than armies, more relentless than death. I think it is this demon which has provided the new thing in Western Man, the insane dynamic which has driven him across the earth to burn and slaughter, loot and rape.

I believe Lawrence laid that ghost, exorcised that demon, once for all, by an act of absolute spiritual transvaluation. "Piano," "Silence," "The Bride," and the other poems of that period, should be read with the tenth chapter of the ninth book of the *Confessions*. It is the beginning and the end. Augustine was a saint. There are acts of salvation by which man can raise himself to heaven, but, say the Japanese, a devil is substituted in his place. Lawrence drove out the devil, and the man stepped back. Or, as the Hindus say, with an act of absolute devotion from the worshiper, the goddess changes her aspect from maleficent to benign.

It is not only that Lawrence opened the gates of personal salvation for himself in the "mother" poems. He did it in a special way, in the only way possible, by an intense realization of total reality, and by the assumption of total responsibility for the reality and for the realization. Other people have tried parts of this process, but only the whole thing

182

works. This shows itself in these poems, in their very technique. There, for the first time, he is in full possession of his faculties. He proceeds only on the basis of the completely real, the completely motivated, step by step along the ladder of Blake's "minute particulars." Ivor Richards' *Practical Criticism* contains a symposium of his students on Lawrence's "Piano." It makes one of the best introductions to Lawrence's poetry ever written. And one of the qualities of his verse that is revealed there most clearly is the uncanny, "surreal" accuracy of perception and evaluation. Objectivism is a hollow word beside this complete precision and purposiveness.

From this time on Lawrence never lost contact with the important thing, the totality in the particular, the responsibility of vision. Harassed by sickness and betrayal, he may have faltered in fulfilling that most difficult of all the injunctions of Christ, to suffer fools gladly. He may have got out of contact with certain kinds of men at certain times. He may have become cross and irritable and sick. But he never lost sight of what really mattered: the blue vein arching over the naked foot, the voices of the fathers singing at the charivari, blending in the winter night, Lady Chatterley putting flowers in Mellors' pubic hair.

The "Helen" poems are strange. (See "A Winter's Tale," "Return," "Kisses in the Train," "Under the Oak," "Passing Visit to Helen," "Release," and "Seven Seals.") They all have a weird, dark atmosphere shot through with spurts of flame, a setting which remained a basic symbolic situation with Lawrence. It is the atmosphere of the pre-War I novel, young troubled love in gas-lit London—draughty, dark, and flaring, and full of mysterious movement. Probably the girl's name was not Helen. Lawrence thought of her as dim, larger than life, a demi-goddess, moving through the smoke of a burning city. For certain Gnostics Helen was the name of the incarnate "female principle," the power of the will, the sheath of the sword, the sacred whore who taught men love. Helen seems to have been the midwife of Lawrence's manhood. At the end, something like her returns in the Persephone of "Bavarian Gentians." Re-birth. No one leaves adolescence cleanly without a foretaste of death.

Ezra Pound said that the dialect poems were the best thing Lawrence ever wrote. This is just frivolous eccentricity. But they are fine poems, and in them another figure of the myth is carefully drawn. They are poems about Lawrence's father, the coal miner who emerges nightly from the earth with the foliage of the carboniferous jungles on his white body. Lawrence's little dark men, his Gypsies, and Indians, and Hungarians, and Mexicans, and all the rest, are not dark by race, but dark with coal dust. The shadow of forests immeasurably older than man has stained their skins. Augustine was never at peace until he found his father again in the pure mental absolute of Plotinus. Lawrence found his father again in the real man, whose feet went down into the earth. In certain poems where he speaks as a fictional woman, the erotic intensity is embarrassing to those of us who still live in the twilight of the Oedipus Complex. What had been evil in the father

image becomes a virtue, the source of the will; deeply behind the mother image lies the germ of action, the motile
flagellate traveling up the dark hot tube, seeking immortality.

The boy watching the miners rise and descend in the
yawning maw of the earth in Nottinghamshire grows into
the man of forty watching the Indians pass in and out of a
lodge where an old man is interminably chanting—there is
a sense of strangeness, but no estrangement. There is no
effort to violate the mystery of paternity because it is known
in the blood. Lawrence knew by a sort of sensual perception
that every cell of his body bore the marks of the striped
Joseph's coat of the paternal sperm.

All this world of the early poems, and of the novels,
*The White Peacock, The Trespasser,* the first draft of *Sons
and Lovers,* is an unborn world, a cave, a womb, obscure
and confused. The figures have a mythic vagueness about
them. The sensual reality seems to be always struggling beneath an inhibiting surface of flesh, struggling to escape
into another realm of meaning. So many of the images are
drawn from birth, escape, confinement, struggle. Critics
have found much of their Freudianism in the work of this
period. Had they been better read they would have found
Jung above all else, and certainly Rank. Lawrence had yet
to read Freud or Jung and may never have heard of Rank.

Some shockingly ill-informed things have been written
about Lawrence's relation to psychoanalysis. In the first
place, he was not a Freudian. He seems to have read little
Freud, not to have understood him any too well, and to

have disliked him heartily. In the winter of 1918–19 he read Jung, apparently for the first time, in English. Presumably this was *The Psychology of the Unconscious*. Jung was very much in the air in those days, as he is again. There was probably a great deal of amateur talk about his ideas among Lawrence's friends. But Lawrence does not seem to have had much more to go on, and *The Psychology of the Unconscious* is only the beginning of the system later elaborated by Jung. Nor did he ever become intimate with any of Jung's students. Later Mabel Dodge tried to bring the two together by correspondence. The story goes that Jung ignored her letters because they were written in pencil. So much for that.

Lawrence wrote quite a bit on psychoanalysis. There are the two books, *Psychoanalysis and the Unconscious*, a somewhat sketchy popularization of some of Jung's basic concepts, and *Fantasia of the Unconscious*, of which more in a moment. And then there are the reviews of Trigant Burrow's book, and miscellaneous remarks scattered through correspondence and reviews. This is all of the greatest importance to the understanding of Lawrence.

*Fantasia of the Unconscious* is an extraordinary book. It is foully written, unquestionably Lawrence's worst writing, but it is certainly a landmark in the history of psychoanalysis. It is an attempt to combine the empirical neurology of Kundalini Yoga with his own interpretation of Jung's psychology and with a theory of sexuality which may be either his own or derived from popular, occultist expositions of certain Gnostic sects and rumors of the practices of Shakti-Yoga. When it appeared, it must have seemed like pure fantasy of the Lost Atlantis variety. Jung's *Secret of the Golden Flower*, and his studies of "spiritual alchemy" lay in the future. The "psychology of the autonomic system" was unheard of. It is all there, in Lawrence's inspired guesses. The white race is going mad, but it is the autonomic nervous system which is out of kilter; what goes on in the head is secondary—and the autonomic nervous system is, as a whole, the organ of communion.

To return to the poems. There is an hallucinatory quality in the images of the poems which precede Frieda which it is interesting to compare with the induced hallucination of H.D. The conflict in H.D. is hidden in herself. It is still there to this day, although her latest prose work has been the journal of a Freudian analysis. Her images are purified of conflict; then the intensity which has been distilled from the sublimation of conflict is applied from the outside. ("Your poetry is not pure, eternal, sublimated," she told Lawrence.) What results is a puzzling hallucination of fact, a contentless mood which seems to reflect something tremendously important but whose mystery always retreats before analysis.

Lawrence's early poems are poems of conflict. The images are always polarized. Antagonisms struggle through the texture. But the struggle is real. The antagonisms are struggling toward the light. The conflict yields to insight, if not to analysis. It is like the propaedeutic symbolism of the dream, as contrasted to the trackless labyrinths of falsifica-

187

tion which form the patterns of most waking lives. The hallucination is real, the vision of the interior, personal oracle. Its utterance has meaning, more meaning than ordinary waking reality because the subjective is seen in the objective, emerging from it, the dream from the reality—not dislocated or applied from outside the context.

The poems of *Look! We Have Come Through* fall into three groups. First there are the structurally more conventional pieces like "Moonrise," which sounds a little like Masefield's sonnets though it is incomparably finer, and the "Hymn to Priapus," and the others—they are all probably earlier and have already been discussed. Second, there are the poems of the Rhine Journey, "December Night," "New Year's Eve," "Coming Awake," "History"; erotic epigrams, intense as Meleager, more wise than Paul the Silentiary. Lawrence was still a young man, and had many great poems to write—but put these beside the few poets who have survived from that day, Sturge Moore, Monro, De La Mare . . . they look like pygmies. Only Yeats stands up against Lawrence. And last, there are the Whitmanic free verse manifestoes, "explaining" marriage to a people who had forgotten what it was.

With Frieda the sleeper wakes, the man walks free, the "child" of the alchemists is born. Reality is totally valued, and passes beyond the possibility of hallucination. The clarity of purposively realized objectivity is the most supernatural of all visions. Bad poetry always suffers from the same defects: synthetic hallucination and artifice. Invention is not poetry. Invention is defense, the projection of pseudopods out of the ego to ward off the "other." Poetry is vision, the pure act of sensual communion and contemplation.

That is why the poems of Lawrence and Frieda on their Rhine Journey are such great poetry. That is why they are also the greatest imagist poems ever written. Reality streams through the body of Frieda, through everything she touches, every place she steps, valued absolutely, totally, beyond time and place, in the minute particular. The swinging of her breasts as she stoops in the bath, the roses, the deer, the harvesters, the hissing of the glacier water in the steep river—everything stands out lit by a light not of this earth and at the same time completely of this earth, the light of the Holy Sacrament of Marriage, whose source is the wedded body of the bride.

The accuracy of Lawrence's observation haunts the mind permanently. I have never stood beside a glacier river, at just that relative elevation, and just that pitch, with just that depth of swift water moving over a cobbled bed, without hearing again the specific hiss of Lawrence's Isar. These poems may not be sublimated (whatever Y.M.C.A. evasion that may refer to), but they are certainly pure and eternal.

Again, it is fruitful to compare the Rhine Journey poems with the only other poems of our time which resemble them much, Ford Madox Ford's *Buckshee*. Ford was writing about something very akin to what Lawrence was, about an aspect of marriage. But he was writing about its impossibility, about how life had bled away its possibility from both him and his girl, and how they had taken, in middle age and in the long Mediterranean drouth, the next best thing—intense erotic friendship. And about how, every once in a while, marriage comes and looks in at the window. The contrast with Lawrence and Frieda, sinking into the twilight in the fuming marsh by the Isar, "where the snake disposes," is pathetic past words.

Ford's "L'Oubli—Temps de Secheresse" and Lawrence's "River Roses" and "Quite Forsaken" are things of a kind and the best of their kind, but like the north and south poles, there is all the difference in the world between them. There is more communion in Frieda's temporary absence than in the closest possible kiss "under the catalpa tree, where the strange birds, driven north by the drouth, cry with their human voices." "Singular birds, with their portentous, singular flight and human voices," says Ford. This is the Persephone of "Bavarian Gentians" and the Orphic birds which flutter around the dying who are withdrawing themselves, corpuscle by corpuscle, from communion. Lawrence would come there one day, with the dark blue flowers on the medicine table and Frieda sleeping in a chair beside him, but he was on the other side of the universe then—the early summer of 1912, in the Isartal, the snow leaving the mountains.

After the Rhine Journey come the poems of struggle for a living adjustment. The ceremonial glory of the sacrament passes from the forefront of consciousness, and the period of adjustment to the background of life begins. Every detail of life must be transformed by marriage. This means creative conflict on the most important level.

Sacramental communion is bound by time. Mass does not last forever. Eventually the communicant must leave the altar and digest the wafer, the Body and Blood must enter his own flesh as it moves through the world and struggles with the devil. The problem lies in the sympathetic nervous system, says Lawrence. And it is not easy for two members of a deranged race, in the twentieth century, to learn again how to make those webs mesh as they should.

Some of these poems are, in a sense, Frieda's—records of her own interior conquest. It is amazing how much they accomplished, these two. Today, revisiting this battlefield between love and hate that is so carefully mapped in certain of the poems, it is like Gettysburg, a sleepy, pastoral landscape dotted with monuments and graves. Only maimed women and frightened men are Suffragettes anymore. Hedda Gabler is dead, or lurking in the suburbs. We should be grateful to Frieda. It was she who gave the dragon its death blow, and the Animus no longer prowls the polls and bedrooms, seeking whom it may devour.

The Whitmanic poems seem to owe a good deal to *Children of Adam and Calamus*. They look like Whitman on the page. But if read aloud with any sort of ear, they don't sound much like him. Whitman flourished in the oratorical context of nineteenth-century America. He isn't rhetorical in the invidious sense; that is, there is nothing covert or coercive about him. He says what he means, but he says it

191

in the language of that lost art of elocution so popular in his day. There is little of this in Lawrence. At this period his long-lined free verse is derived almost entirely from the poetry of the Bible, the Psalms, the song of Deborah, the song of Hezekiah, of Moses, the Benedicite, the Magnificat, the Nunc Dimitus. All the devices of Hebrew poetry are there, and in addition the peculiar, very civilized, self-conscious, "sympathetic" poetry of St. Luke—those poems which have made his the "women's Gospel," and which all good Englishmen must learn in childhood as part of the Morning and Evening Prayer of the Church.

In the volume *Look! We Have Come Through* Lawrence was just beginning to learn to write free verse. I don't think some of the poems are completely successful. They are diffuse and long-winded. He tries to say too much, and all at the same pitch of intensity; there are no crises, no points of reference. On the whole the most successful is "New Heaven and Earth." It may not be a perfect object of art but it is a profound exhortation.

Beyond Holy Matrimony lies the newly valued world of birds, beasts, and flowers—a sacramentalized, objective world. "Look, we have come through"—to a transformed world, with a glory around it everywhere like ground lightning. The poems of *Birds, Beasts, and Flowers* have the same supernatural luster that shines through the figures of men and animals and things, busy being part of a new redeemed world, as they are found carved around the mandala of the Blessed Virgin above some cathedral door or on some rose window.

*Birds, Beasts, and Flowers* is the mature Lawrence, in complete control of his medium, or completely controlled by his demon. He never has any trouble. He can say exactly what he wants to say. Except for the death poems, he would never write better. (And too, after this, he would never be well again.) He seems to have lived in a state of total realization—the will and its power, positive and negative, at maximum charge, and all the universe streaming between them glowing and transformed. The work of art grows in that electric field, is a "function" of it. It is the act of devotion in the worshiper that forces the god to occupy the statue. It is the act of devotion in the sculptor that forces the god to occupy the stone which the artist then pares to his invisible limbs, tailors like cloth. It is never theology in the first; it is never aesthetics or any teachable craft in the second. The craft is the vision and the vision is the craft.

Good cadenced verse is the most difficult of all to write. Any falsity, any pose, any corruption, any ineptitude, any vulgarity, shows up immediately. In this it is like abstract painting. A painting by Mondrian may look impersonal enough to be reduced to code and sent by telegraph. Maybe. But it offers no refuge, no garment, no mask, no ambush, for the person. The painter must stand there, naked, as Adam under the eye of God. Only very great or very trivial personalities dare expose themselves so.

Think of a few typical writers of cadenced verse: Whitman, Sandburg, Wallace Gould, F. M. Ford, F. S. Flint, Aldington, Lola Ridge, and James Oppenheim. (H.D.'s verse is primarily a counterpointing of accentual and quantitative rhythms in patterns of Greek derivation. Pound's verse is Latin in reference, and usually quantitative.) How the faults stand out! Every little weakness is revealed with glaring cruelty. Whitman's tiresome posturing, Sandburg's mawkishness, Aldington's erotic sentimentality, the over-reaching ambition of Lola Ridge and Oppenheim—what a lot of sore thumbs standing out! Yet in many ways these are good poets, and Whitman is a very great one.

Gould, Flint, and Ford were never dishonest, never over-reached themselves, did their best to say what they meant and no more, never bargained with art. "The sentimental-ist," said Daedalus, "is he who would enjoy, without incur-ring the immense debtorship for a thing done." They are not prophets, but they are good poets because they rendered a strict accounting with their own souls.

Sentimentality is spiritual realization on the installment plan. Socially viable patterns, like conventional verse, are a sort of underwriting or amortization of the weaknesses of the individual. This is the kernel of sense in the hollow snobbery of Valéry. The sonnet and quatrain are like the national debt, devices for postponing the day of reckoning indefinitely. All artistic conventions are a method of spirit-ual deficit-financing. If they were abandoned, the entire credit structure of Poets, Ltd., would be thrown into hope-less confusion. It is just as well that the professors have led the young, in my lifetime, away from free verse to some-thing that can be taught. No one could be taught to be Law-rence, but in a world where the led lead the leaders, those who might pretend to do so are sure to be confidence men.

194

Lawrence's free verse in *Birds, Beasts, and Flowers* is among the small best ever written. It can be analyzed, but the paradigms produced by the analysis are worthless. It cannot be explained away, demonstrated in a mathematical sense. Neither, certainly, can any other great poetry; but at least a convincing illusion can be created, and the young can be provided with something to practice. A poem like "Bat" or the "Lion of St. Mark" moves with a stately, gripping sonority through the most complex symphonic evolutions. The music is a pattern of vibration caught from the resonant tone of Lawrence himself. The concerto is not on the page, little spots with flags and tails on a stave, but the living thing, evolving from the flesh of the virtuoso. It is like Gregorian chant or Hindu music, one thing when sung at Solesmes, or in the ruins of Konarak, another when "rendered" by the Progressive Choral Group or at a concert of the Vedanta Society of Los Angeles.

Again, the faults of *Birds, Beasts, and Flowers* are the excess of virtue. Like anyone who knows he has something intensely important to say, Lawrence found it hard to keep from being long-winded. I think a good deal of his over-expansiveness and repetition is due to his methods of composition.

Some poets meditate in stillness and inactivity, as far away as possible from the creative act. We know that Baudelaire and T. S. Eliot, by their own testimony, spent long periods of time quiescent, inert as artists, turning over and over the substance of vision within themselves. Sometimes, as in Baudelaire, this process is extremely painful, a

195

true desert of the soul. Months went by in which the paper and pen were red hot, it was impossible for him to read, his whole personality seemed engulfed in a burning neurasthenia. And then there would come a period of peace, and slowly growing exaltation, and finally the creative act, almost somnambulistic in its completion. Actual composition by this sort of personality tends to be rare, and usually as perfect as talent permits.

Lawrence meditated pen in hand. His contemplation was always active, flowing out in a continuous stream of creativity which he seemed to have been able to open practically every day. He seldom reversed himself, seldom went back to rework the same manuscript. Instead, he would lay aside a work that dissatisfied him and rewrite it all from the beginning. In his poetry he would move about a theme, enveloping it in constantly growing spheres of significance. It is the old antithesis: centrifugal versus centripetal, Parmenides versus Heraclitus. He kept several manuscript books of his verse, and whenever he wanted to publish a collection he would go through them and pick out a poem here and there, the ones he considered had best handled their themes. Behind each poem was usually a group of others devoted to the same material. His selection was always personal, and sometimes it was not very "artistic." *Nettles*, for instance, is a selection of what are, by any standard, the poorer poems of the collections of epigrams printed in *Last Poems*.

There are those who think these epigrams, the ones in *Pansies*, and those in *Last Poems*, aren't art. This opinion is the product of a singular provincialism. It is true that, due to the reasons just mentioned, they aren't all successful, but they belong to a tradition, are members of a species, which has produced some of the greatest poetry. Epigram or maxim, Martial or La Rochefoucauld, the foundations of this tradition are far more stable than those of the neo-metaphysical poetry produced, with seven ambiguities carefully inserted in every line, by unhappy dons between the wars.

Any bright young man can be taught to be artful. It is impossible to teach taste, but you can teach most anybody caution. It is always the lesser artists who are artful, they must learn their trade by rote. They must be careful never to make a false step, never to speak out of a carefully synthesized character. The greater poetry is nobly disheveled. At least it never shows the scars of taking care. "Would he had blotted a thousand lines," said Ben Jonson of Shakespeare. Which thousand? Lawrence was always mislaying those manuscript books of poetry and writing around the world for them, just as Cézanne left his paintings in the fields. Not for any stupid reason—that they were not Perfect Works of Art—but simply because he forgot.

Eliot (who does not write that way), writing of Pound's epigrams, points out that the major poet, unlike the minor, is always writing about everything imaginable, and so is in good form for the great poem when it comes. Practice makes perfect, and those who wait for the perfect poem before putting pen to paper may wait mute forever. I suppose it is the absolutism which swept over popular taste in

197

the wake of Cubism that has encouraged the ignorant to expect a canzone of Dante's in each issue of their favorite little magazine, a School of Athens in every WPA mural. This is just greediness, like children who want it to be Christmas every day. And it produces an empty, pretentious, greedy art. Meanwhile, Pound's "Les Millwin," and Lawrence's "Willy Wet-Legs," quietly pre-empt immortality, a state of being only rarely grandiose.

As far as I know the poems in the novel *The Plumed Serpent* have never been printed separately. This book is one of the most important (he thought it the most important) Lawrence ever wrote. It has brought forth all sorts of pointless debate. People are always saying: "Well, I have lived in Mexico for years and it *simply* isn't like that." Lawrence was not an idiot. He knew it wasn't. And in the first chapter he gave a very accurate and pitiful picture of the "real" Mexico—sterile, subcolonial, brutal, with the old gods gone, and the church gone, and the revolution a swindle, and nothing left but a squalid imitation of Ashtabula, Ohio. And he knew the other side too, the pasty frigid nymphomaniacs, the deranged women of Europe and America, who consider themselves disciples of Lawrence and prowl the earth seeking Dark Gods to take to bed. He wrote a story which should have destroyed them forever—"None of That." It should be read with *The Plumed Serpent*.

Every year there is less, but in Lawrence's day there was still something, of the primeval Mexico—at the great feast in Oaxaca, in the life of the peasants in the remote villages, in the Indian communities in the back country. Lawrence did not make any very definite contact with the ancient Mexico but he could see and sense it, and he was fresh from a much less-touched primitive world—that of the Navaho and Pueblo Indians of the Southwest. His materials were not as abundant as they might have been but they were enough to build a book of ritual, of the possible that would never be, of potentialities that would never emerge. It is a book of ceremonial prophecy, but prophecy uttered in the foreknowledge that it would never be fulfilled.

The reawakening of mystery, the revival of the old Aztec religion, the political "Indianism"—even if it all came true, one knows it would be a fraud, a politician's device, as Indianism is in Latin America today. Lawrence knew that, of course, and so the book is dogged with tragedy. One constantly expects the characters to go out in a blazing *Götterdämmerung* in some dispute with the police, like a gangster movie. They don't, but maybe it would have been better if they had, for eventually they tire; they seem to become secretly aware that all this gorgeous parading around in primitive millinery, this Mystery, and Fire, and Blood, and Darkness, has been thought up. There is something Western European, British Museum, about it. The protagonist, Kate, submits to her lover's insistent Mystery, but rather out of ennui and loathing of Europe than out of any conviction, and one feels that the book could have no sequel, or only a sequel of disintegration, like *Women in Love*.

Still, in the middle of the book, before the fervor dies out, Lawrence wrote as nearly as he could what he believed should be. If the religion of Cipriano and Ramon is taken as an other-worldly system of values, it is profound and true, and, due to the freshness of its symbols, tremendously exciting. Also, it differs very little from any other religion that has maintained its contacts with its sources. Ramon and Cipriano short-circuit themselves where Christianity was short-circuited by Constantine, in the desire to have both worlds, to found a political religion—a Church. That, if any, is the "message" of the book.

The mystery survives in the poems, just as the sacraments survived Constantine. They are not the greatest poems Lawrence ever wrote, but they are among the most explicit. This is Lawrence's religion. Wherever he found it he is now in complete possession of a kind of orthodoxy, the orthodoxy of the heterodox—the symbolic world of the Gnostics, the Occultists, Tantrism, Jung. In a sense they are failures, these poems, in the way that the Indian songs published by the United States Bureau of Ethnology are not failures. But, again, that is the message of the book. Finally you discover that you cannot make up paganism. What you make up is a cult. There is nothing primitive about Gnosticism, anymore than there is anything primitive about Theosophy. It is the creation of over-civilized Hellenistic intellectuals. Tantrism too grew up in India, in Buddhism and Hinduism, when civilization was exhausting itself. Jung comes, with Lawrence, at the end of the career of Western European Man. Lawrence, after all, was a contemporary of Niels Bohr and Picasso. And so his poems are mystical poems—and the Aztecs were not mystics, they were just Aztecs. This doesn't invalidate the poems. They have very little to do with ancient or modern Mexico, but they do express, very well, the personal religion of D. H. Lawrence. They may be full of "occult lore," but behind the machinery is an intense, direct, personal, mystical apprehension of reality.

In the last hours Lawrence seems to have lived in a state of suspended animation, removed from the earth, floating, transfigured by the onset of death. Poems like "Andraitix," "Pomegranate Flowers," have an abstracted, disinterested intensity, as though they were written by a being from another planet. Others are short mystical apothegms. There is no millinery anymore, no occultism; they differ only in their modern idiom from any and all of the great mystics. And finally there are the two death poems, "Bavarian Gentians" and "The Ship of Death." Each was written over several times. There exists a variant which can be taken as a final, or pre-final, version of "Bavarian Gentians," but both are clusters of poems rather than finished products.

"The Ship of Death" material alone would make a small book of meditations, a contemporary *Holy Dying*. It is curious to think that once such a book would have been a favorite gift for the hopelessly ill. Today people die in hospitals, badgered by nurses, stupefied with barbiturates. This is not an age in which a "good death" is a desired end of life.

All men have to die, and one would think a sane man would want to take that fact into account, at least a little. But our whole civilization is a conspiracy to pretend that it

201

isn't going to happen—and this, in an age when death has become more horrible, more senseless, less at the will of the individual than ever before. Modern man is terribly afraid of sex, of pain, of evil, of death. Today childbirth, the ultimate orgiastic experience, has been reduced to a meaningless dream; dentists insist on injecting Novocain before they clean your teeth; the agonies of life have retreated to the source of life. Men and women torture each other to death in the bedroom, just as the dying dinosaurs gnawed each other as they copulated in the chilling marshes. Anything but the facts of life. Today you can take a doctor's degree in medicine or engineering and never learn how to have intercourse with a woman or repair a car. Human self-alienation, Marx called it. He said that was all that was really wrong with capitalism. "Let us live and lie reclined" in a jet-propelled, streamlined, air-cooled, lucite incubator. When we show signs of waking, another cocktail instead of the Wine of God. When we try to break out, flagellation instead of Holy Matrimony, psychoanalysis instead of Penance. When the machinery runs down, morphine for Extreme Unction.

In a world where death had become a nasty, pervasive secret like defecation or masturbation, Lawrence re-instated it in all its grandeur—the oldest and most powerful of the gods. "The Ship of Death" poems have an exaltation, a nobility, a steadiness, an insouciance, which is not only not of this time but is rare in any time. It doesn't matter who: Jeremy Taylor, the Orphic Hymns, the ancient Egyptians—nobody said it better. And there is one aspect of the "Ship of Death" which is unique. Lawrence did not try to mislead himself with false promises, imaginary guarantees. Death is the absolute, unbreakable mystery. Communion and oblivion, sex and death, the mystery can be revealed—but it can be revealed only as totally inexplicable. Lawrence never succumbed to the temptation to try to do more. He succeeded in what he did do.

# TURNER:
# PAINTING AS AN
# ORGANISM OF LIGHT

Until recently, when a wholesale revision of reputations and change of taste set in in the arts, people who prided themselves on being up-to-date looked patronizingly back on Turner as an artist for adolescents. Today, when it has become fashionable for a painter to speak of himself as a romantic abstract-expressionist, Turner is coming back into favor.

I think these attitudes point up certain more obvious qualities of his work—probably faults rather than virtues. They may both be summed up in one generalization: Turner was a plebeian artist with thoroughly plebeian tastes.

Taste can be a great obstacle to the appreciation of painting, as is obvious again in Turner's polar opposite, William Blake. It makes or breaks second-rate work, but it has little to do with the very greatest paintings, or at least painters. Cézanne, for instance, had no taste whatever. Turner's positive passion for trees with silky silhouettes, sunsets no artist could paint, snowstorms in the Alps that beat about the head of Livy's Hannibal, storms at sea that beset Captain Kidd, seems a little ingenuous and boyish to sensibilities corrupted by a century of black bile, alienation, and world ill.

Many people still think of Turner in terms of the repro-
duction which hung on the wall in high school. Before
approaching him as a serious artist it is necessary to over-
come a natural modern distaste for his taste. It would be
easier for most people if he had painted ugly pictures. We
have been taught to look through and past the ugly. Unfortunately he painted very pretty pictures indeed, prettier
than Russell Flint or Leon Kroll.

Once the initial shudder of repugnance is past, it becomes apparent that Turner was not only one of the climac-
teric painters, a genuine original and an undying influence,
but that his plastic notions, his idea of space, and the ends
which he envisaged as possible in painting are peculiarly
modern—modern in this case meaning something very
different from the Cubist-Classicism of the first quarter of
the century or the psychologism of the second.

I am not going to talk about Turner's more famous paintings—the illustrative and picturesque landscapes, the
heroic compositions, the battle pieces, and the sentimental
anecdotes, like the *Téméraire* or *Sea Burial of Wilkie*. I
think most of these are very great paintings. The last is a
spectacular abstract composition in red, grey, and black.
But they are endangered by their obvious appeal. Instead I
shall try to trace, in terms of pictures most of which can
be found in collections of reproductions, the evolution of
Turner not only as an abstract artist but as a painter who
was working towards a vision of a kind of space unknown
in the Occident. Tintoretto and Tiepolo had preceded him,
but their achievements were not understood. Turner's were

not to be understood either. The nineteenth century appreciated him for his romantic, picturesque landscapes, the Impressionists for his divided and brilliant color, the early twentieth century smiled patronizingly.

Speaking of his color and of the necessity of discussing him as a painter in books, it happens that Turner had very little respect for his métier, or at least no knowledge of color chemistry. Practically all of the few paintings in American collections bear little resemblance to their original state. In mid life he began to take more care. Even so, hundreds of his paintings had disintegrated or faded hopelessly by the time of his death. The best are in the great Turner galleries in the Tate, in the National Gallery, and in a few English private collections. There are, though, many volumes of excellent color reproductions in any well-stocked public library.

I don't want to talk about Turner's technical means and his mastery of them. He was one of the first artists to use divided color consistently. He was one of the first artists to use pure spectrum color. He was one of the first artists to think of a painting as what has come to be called an abstraction. But these items in the history of art we have all learned in high school. Any revolutionary decorator could have accomplished as much. He is more important than this.

Leaving aside for a moment the main development of Turner's art, I would like to say something about an aspect of his life which has always embarrassed his British biographers and critics—his attitude toward people and toward

206

sex. His human figures have a strange inhumanity. This is something that seems to have been a late-eighteenth-century convention. They are like Longhi but less doll-like, more perhaps like Goya than anyone else, whose *Spain, Time, and History* (1799) might have been painted by Turner. This is an attitude towards people which will lead eventually to Giacometti or Tanguy, or, for that matter, Nadelman. These figures are the androids of science fiction —*Between Decks* (1827, Tate); *Jessica* (around 1830, Collection of Lord Leconfield, Petworth)—one of the most startlingly human figures in the world's art, she looks for all the world like a visitor popping her head out of a flying saucer; and the large, red, unfinished nude in the Tate, which certainly has none of the appearance of a calendar girl but is one of the hottest pictures ever painted —so much so that it is positively difficult to look at. I happen to have seen it the same day I saw Boucher's *La Petite Morphi*, which was in London on loan at the time and which is a very great painting in its own right. No chasm separates these two women, but a whole universe. I don't wonder that Turner couldn't finish it. But as far as he went he painted one of the world's most unforgettable thoughts.

With these pictures, which all seem to have been painted at Petworth around 1830, it is convenient to place *The Room at Petworth* (1830, British Museum), because of its color—red—and its treatment of interior light—shafts and whorls of sun motes. It is the most fashionable of Turner's

207

paintings nowadays, one of his greatest, and the first intimation of the purely visionary style of his last years.

Looking into a book of Turner will impart something of the same sensation, but nothing can compare with walking into the great Turner galleries of the Tate. The sensation is not an aesthetic one but a human one. You feel immersed in the very being of a personality. It is like acquiring all at once a life-time of a close family relationship. The ideal classical painting is as impersonal as Poussin—the person simply does not exist behind the canvas. A gallery full of Poussins would be a gallery full of independent objects of art which might just as well have grown naturally like crystals. Only the full impact of room after room of intensely personal and expressionistic paintings like Turner's can bring home the full meaning of expressionism, personalism.

It is this personal power and personal integrity, fully as much as the plastic originality, which almost immediately override Turner's taste.

It is interesting to compare Blake and Turner. Once again, like Poe and Whitman, the culture reveals its polarity. Both of them were tasteless artists, yet with Palmer and Calvert they are the leading painters of Great Britain. They were tasteless artists because good taste was not so much bad as trivial. They were plebeian artists and upstarts because official society was not so much vicious or dishonest as stereotyped. This is not always necessarily true, but looking back on the nineteenth and late eighteenth centuries, it is easy to believe that it has been.

Blake drew, rather than painted, objects in empty space. His work was a sort of small hypertrophy of the principles of Renaissance art. He was to Marcantonio as Marcantonio was to Raphael or Michelangelo—a reduction in scale, an increase in specialization. With all his hatred of Newton, he was an eminently Newtonian painter. Doubtless he would have hated Machiavelli too, but the figures of his mythology, whether plastic or literary, were isolated Renaissance men struggling with each other for mastery— Job, Los, Enitharmon, Satan are figures like the Borgias and the Medicis.

Turner painted, at least in his maturity, dynamic saturated space, all the forces of which were organically related like the strains and stresses, the vacuoles, vortices, and pseudopods which make up the living processes of an amoeba. Even in the heroic paintings, Ulysses is a scrawl of color, Polyphemus a cloud.

Both Turner and Blake started out as artists for the engraver and continued such work all their lives. Blake's excited polemic for outline, silhouette, sharp planes of black and white, is known to everyone. As for Turner, Pye, his best engraver, said, "The one great aim of landscape art is to enable the spectator to see, as it were, into space; and this can be done only by a perfect knowledge of light."

This is a description of emotional or even spiritual phenomena, rather than a statement of fact. If one compares Turner and his engravers with the work of Stothard and Blake, or even better with the contemporary French and Italian mezzotint and steel engravers, it is apparent that he

209

was practically the inventor of the romantic vista which was to ornament the fine books of a century—the long receding stage sets of tonalities, late afternoon light shining through the whole meteorological collection of cloud forms —so different from the building-block landscapes, the cones, cylinders, and cubes, the representation of great mass, typical of the classical tradition as seen in Poussin. And, of course, different from the linear art of the best French engravers.

It is very seldom that an artist realizes immediately upon its invention the possibilities of a medium as Turner did those of steel engraving. The mezzotint technique of the *Liber Studiorum* approaches the later attitude toward light, but the medium sets definite limits—the limits, say, of the landscapes of Claude Lorrain or Rubens. The contrast of dark and light still looks suspiciously technical—*sfumato*.

All his life Turner painted Norham Castle. Compare the early paintings with the famous watercolor of 1835, the mezzotint of the *Liber Studiorum* with the engraving. This attitude toward reality as a complex of vortices of pure light reaches its height in the engravings in pictures like *Llanthony Abbey* (1835) in the *England and Wales* series.

The next step plastically is *A Storm in the Mountains*, once in the Darrell Brown collection but painted before 1810. Only the lower-right sixth of the painting contains some trees and cows. The rest is a turbulence of mingled rock, cloud, and light.

By 1835, one of Turner's great years, many of the paintings and most of the watercolors have moved close to abstraction. This is the year of *Sunrise, A Boat Between Headlands, Hastings,* and the most abstract *Norham Castle.* From this point on, Turner moved steadily toward perfect mastery of a new vision.

It is exciting to take another subject like Norham Castle and trace it down the years: *St. Gothard Pass* in the *Liber Studiorum.* The sketches and watercolors of 1802, 1803, culminating in the *Pass of St. Gothard Near Faido* (1843), once in Ruskin's collection and now, as I remember, in the Tate. The last is like nothing else in the world of art except Turner. This is the light metaphysics of the neo-Platonists and the medieval mystics. In paintings like this, Turner may not be a greater painter than Sesshu, Ying Yu-Chien, Hsia Kuei, the dragon painters, Tintoretto, or Tiepolo. But he has fully understood the nature of his vision—certainly more fully than any Western European artist except Tintoretto or Tiepolo. The principal difference with Turner is, again, this time on a very high level, his plebeian taste. His concept of space is the same as Sesshu's. It is simply more simple-minded, less refined and less complex. In other words, less goes on in it and what does is more obvious.

I should say that the great paintings always to be found on exhibit in the Turner galleries of the Tate or the National Gallery and all reproduced somewhere in color are *The Burning of the Ships* (after 1840, Tate), *Snow Storm at Sea* (1842, National Gallery), *Rain, Steam, and Speed* (1844, National Gallery), *Sunrise with Sea Monster* (1845, Tate), *Mercury and Argus* (1836, Tate), *Juliet and Her Nurse* (1836, Tate), *Sea Piece* (1842, once in the Orrock

Collection), and finally the great visionary paintings of his last years, his seventies, culminating in *An Angel in the Sun* (1846, Tate), *Queen Mab's Cave* (1846, National Gallery), *Mercury Sent to Admonish Aeneas* (1850, Tate), *Aeneas and Dido* (1850, Tate), *Departure of the Trojan Fleet* (1850, Tate), and *The Visit to the Tomb* (1850, Tate).

These are not just paintings of a special vision. They are visionary paintings of a transcendence curiously like Blake at his best, but the work of an incomparably more knowledgeable painter.

It is remarkable how un-Western-European Turner was. He lived all his life in great simplicity, with his working-man father, and two successive mistresses who were both illiterate. He amassed an immense fortune and left it, with all his paintings, the best of which he had refused to sell, to his native country and to charity. (His will was broken by remote and greedy heirs.)

His life was an imperturbable march toward an always growing light—that reality peculiarly Turner's—and an ever increasing mastery of the means of expressing that vision.

There is not the slightest trace in his life of artistic vanity or worldly ambition. In the sense in which the Greek philosophers meant it, in the sense of Lao-tze, he lived unknown.

# THE CHINESE
# CLASSIC NOVEL
# IN TRANSLATION

## THE ART OF MAGNANIMITY

Grove Press has just issued Pearl Buck's classic translation, *All Men Are Brothers*.* They also import Clement Egerton's translation of *The Golden Lotus*. This is the *Ching P'ing Mei* which is in print in another, somewhat more abridged translation, published by Putnam's. World is reputedly thinking about reprinting the excessively scarce Brewitt-Taylor translation of *San Kuo, the Romance of Three Kingdoms*. Lin Yutang's translation of *Six Chapters of a Floating Life* is available in the Modern Library Giant, *The Wisdom of China and India* (perhaps the best book bargain in America, as this story is certainly Lin Yutang's best work). I hope Arthur Waley's *Monkey* is still in print. Now Pantheon is bringing out the greatest of all Chinese novels, *The Dream of the Red Chamber*,† early next year. This takes care of all the major works of Chinese fiction except Herbert Giles' *Strange Stories from a Chinese Studio* and Jackson's translation of *All Men Are*

---

* Grove Press, N.Y., 1957. 2 vols.
† Translated from Franz Kuhn's German translation of the Chinese by Florence and Isabel McHugh. Pantheon Books, N.Y., 1958.

*Brothers,* which he titled *The Water Margin.* (This is close to the Chinese title; Pearl Buck's was her own idea.)

There are a few other odds and ends. Various Chinese erotic tales are available in pocket books and fugitive "esoteric press" editions. The fiction volume of the two-volume *Chinese Prose Literature of the Tang Period,* translated by E. D. Edwards and published by Probsthain in London, might well be dressed up more attractively, given a new introduction, and imported into America. H. Bedford Jones, of all people, once translated from the French of George Soulié de Morant three Chinese novels, *The Claws of the Dragon, The Passion of Yang Kuei Fei,* and *The Breeze in the Moonlight.* They could all bear reissue, the last especially. Anyway, within the year, anybody who wants to bother can get himself a pretty good picture of Chinese classical fiction.

And what sort of picture is this? What kind of novels are they? To borrow the critical techniques of my colleague, Mr. Yvor Winters, for a moment, they are great novels, very great novels. In fact I would say that *The Dream of the Red Chamber* and the Japanese *Tale of Genji* are the two greatest works of prose fiction in all the history of literature, and that all the others belong on anybody's list of 100 Best Books. That they are not on the Hutchins-Adler list is an excellent indicator of the Western, Thomism-cum-Whiggery parochialism of Mr. Hutchins and Mr. Adler. I am not trying to be odd or annoying. I am not saying something like "Sturge Moore is the greatest poet of the twentieth century." I really do believe that these are

214

the two best novels in the world. Furthermore, there are not many people who are familiar with them who do not agree with me. *The Tale of Genji* is worth a long essay in itself, and besides, its virtues are curiously almost the exact opposite of those characteristic of the greatest Chinese fiction.

What are these virtues? First, an absolute mastery of pure narrative. Second, humanity. Third, as the synthesis of virtues one and two, a whole group of qualities that should have some one name—reticence, artistic humility, maturity, objectivity, total sympathy, the ability to reveal the macrocosm in the microcosm, the moral universe in the physical act, the depths of psychological insight in the trivia of happenstance, without ever saying anything about it, or them—the "big" things, that is. This is a quality of style. It is the fundamental quality of the greatest style. It does have a name, although it is not a term we usually think of as part of the jargon of literary criticism. The word is magnanimity.

The antonym, I guess, is self-indulgence. Surely one of the characteristics of our naughty age is the self-indulgence of our artists, and none more so than our novelists. "Modern classic" or vulgar trash, my usual reaction to a novel full of cocktail party psychoanalysis and indigestible recipes from the latest stylistic cookbooks is, "Oh, for God's sake, come off it. Grown men don't behave this way." And who isn't self-indulgent? Proust? Henry James? The author of *Finnegans Wake*? Jack Kerouac? Jean Stafford? To ask the question, as they say in speeches, is to answer it.

215

I know of only one completely adult major novel of my time, Ford Madox Ford's Tietjens series, reissued a couple of years ago by Knopf with the title *Parade's End*. It is significant that it was badly reviewed and then remaindered, partly because the introduction by an American professor and the publicity by the Knopf staff demonstrated a one hundred per cent incomprehension of its significance. Nobody realized that it was the most important twentieth-century "war novel" in any language; nobody even knew what it was about: that war is the hypertrophy and social proliferation of tiny, trivial, sordid, personal evil—what grandma used to call sin. Ford didn't label his thesis; he probably didn't know he had one in that sense. His characters didn't philosophize about it. He didn't snoop around in their minds with a lot of jargon. Nobody's consciousness streamed. It all just happened, like it does, and you were left with that—the brutal and the silly and the beautiful facts. It is so easy to be artistic. It is so hard to be mature. This is not a digression. This is the very essence of the Chinese novel. Magnanimity.

During the Second World War I knew a little old Quaker from a farm in Indiana who traveled around the country at his own expense and got up in First Day meetings to recite Webster's definition of magnanimity. He had "come with this concern to thee, because thee might find it helpful." This is the definition:

"*magnanimity*, n.; pl.—ties. (F. magnanimité, L. magnanimitas.) 1. Quality of being magnanimous; that quality or combination of qualities in character

216

enabling one to encounter danger and trouble with tranquility and firmness, to disdain injustice, meanness, and revenge, and to act and sacrifice for noble objects. 2. A deed or a disposition characterized by magnanimity. 3. Grandiose temperament; extravagance of soul. Rare."

Having said that the little old Quaker sat down and next week appeared at another meeting. It certainly did help me, probably more than any other words in those hideous years.

No artist belongs in the very first rank who is the victim of his creations. Only this special kind of nobility guaranteed the independence of the primary creators. Homer has it, but Dante does not. It is a kind of courage, like Johnson's famous "Courage, Sir, is the first of virtues, because without it, it is sometimes difficult to exercise the others."

To a degree, no one, in the classic days of Far Eastern civilization, even tried to become an artist of any kind unless he had a little of this magnanimity, this courage. The whole pattern of the culture, the definition and discipline of "human heartedness," was set to produce this kind of character above all others. It is the rarest trait in a predatory, commercial society of human self-alienation, where indeed, covetousness is number one in the decalogue of social virtues, not number ten of the Ten Commandments, and courage—well, it certainly increases sales resistance.

Narrative integrity means that the meanings of a major Chinese novel emerge as revelations, as the meaning of a Sung vase is revealed. Coming on a book like *All Men Are*

*Brothers* for the first time, the unprepared Western reader may think he has wandered into a sort of Chinese "Dick Tracy" or "Terry and the Pirates." In the first place, what's wrong with Dick Tracy? To ape Mr. Winters again, he is certainly "better" than Françoise Sagan, he may even be better than much bigger reputations. And who is so hard-hearted that he did not weep over the death of the Dragon Lady? And who so soft-headed that he wept over the troubles of Albertine? There is only one trouble with Dick Tracy—no important revelation emerges. There is nothing wrong with the novels of Ernest Haycox. This is the best way to write, but something more important emerges from Homer or *The Red and the Black* or *War and Peace* or *Robinson Crusoe* or *Huckleberry Finn*—something false emerges from most twentieth-century novels.

Alex Comfort compares the style of the *Ching P'ing Mei* to Pepys—"a perfectly translucent medium through which we see the characters in all their moral nudity."

*All Men Are Brothers* is the story of the adventures of a gang of quasi-revolutionary brigands of the type who have flourished during all the many periods when Chinese civilization fell on evil days. While they were out, the book was very popular with the Chinese Reds. After they came to power it was frowned on for a while. It is dangerous to an extreme. It is at least as episodic as the funny papers. In fact, the first "comic books" in history are precisely children's picture books of the *San Kuo* and *All Men Are Brothers*. You can buy them in Chinatown and illustrate your own copies. It is chock full of ghosts, innkeepers who

218

make hamburgers of their guests, giants of superhuman strength, beautiful women in distress, wily intellectuals, crafty merchants, tireless lechers, heroic gluttons, sensitive scholars, arson, rape, murder, hairbreadth escapes, pitiful deaths. It is like life, but many times as large. Out of it have grown whole Chinese novels, each as long again. The *Ching P'ing Mei* is simply the elaboration of one episode from *All Men Are Brothers*. From it, as from the *San Kuo*, in fact from all these novels, have been drawn innumerable plays, the favorites of the Chinese theater. Dozens of Western novels could vanish in it without leaving a trace. To produce something like it would require the collaboration of Rabelais, Petronius, Defoe, and Dickens, with, I suppose, details from I. Babel. I do not mean that the author of *All Men Are Brothers* was a "greater" writer than these great Western writers in a qualitative sense, but he certainly was in a quantitative one.

At first maybe it all seems just episodes, something for children, and then slowly the terrific bulk of its humanity begins to creep up on you—that immense Chinese humanity that would never stop coming if it marched past you ten abreast. It is like something in modern astronomy with its multitudes of universes stretching on and on forever. What was it Kant said about the moral law within and the starry heavens without? Here they are, combined, extension and intension, the incredible bulk of the whole human heart. It is like a total recall of your ancestry back to Pekin Man.

When I was a kid, I used to read novels by sets: Tolstoy, Conrad, James, Dostoevski, Turgenev, Zola, Flaubert.

They weren't one book at a time, but a whole world that would envelop me for months and from which I would emerge into real life with the strange outlandish feeling of someone back from years abroad. One Chinese novel can do this to you, sweep you away out of sight of home and self, and lose you for a week or more in its own pullulating verisimilitude.

It is this total verisimilitude which differentiates the greatest Chinese novels from the Japanese and puts *The Dream of the Red Chamber* in a nobler class than *Genji*. The Japanese novel is a universe of exquisite sensibility. It is concerned with the most profound moral issues ever undertaken in any work of fiction, and implicitly with philosophical issues utterly beyond the grasp of any European novelist. It handles all this with breathtaking skill. But it is possible, immediately, to say these things about it. They are patent. You are unaware of anything like this in *The Dream of the Red Chamber* until the week after you have laid it down. You are always aware of the vertiginously beautiful style of Lady Murasaki. In *The Dream of the Red Chamber*, you are unaware you are reading, and nobody remembers who the author was. It is the difference, on a much lesser plane, between Walter Pater and Theodore Dreiser. Dreiser is horribly crude, but Pater is barbarous. I am afraid Dreiser is the better stylist. In *Genji* they eat but seldom, drink a little, but never move their bowels. In the Chinese novel, as in the gardens of Italy where the nightingale sings in the blooming pomegranate, the odor of the night soil of ten thousand years is never out of your nose.

Although they are not so fractious and colorful, there are almost as many characters in *The Dream of the Red Chamber* as there are in *All Men Are Brothers*, and since the *Red Chamber* is not at all episodic, really, but as carefully structured as *The Remembrance of Things Past* or *Genji*, it is easy at first to get lost. But again, in that Chinese way, all these people slowly envelop you with their significance.

What is it all about? It is the story of an idle scholar and gentleman and his women. It is the Chinese plot of plots: "When women rule, the house decays." Again, it is exactly the opposite: a glorification of the hidden matriarchy at the heart of Chinese society. It is the story, I suppose in some sense the plot of all great fiction, of the slow, hard achievement of personal integrity. It is the story of a "Precious Stone," a Taoist saint who doesn't know he is one and doesn't want to be one. There is a distinct resemblance to *Genji*, but a resemblance distinguished by two basically unlike philosophies. Prince Genji (the Shining One) is a hidden Bodhisattva. Now a Bodhisattva is a Buddha who, on the verge of Nirvana, turns away with a vow that he will not enter peace until all sentient creatures have been helped by him to salvation. The Shingon Buddhist doctrine is that he is "indifferent" to this vow. All things are alike to him—but still he does turn away to save others. (This is the explanation for that sort of man-about-town expression on the faces of Japanese statues which looks so unreligious

221

to Westerners.) Lady Murasaki's special contribution was the idea that Genji is not only indifferent, but that he is ignorant of his cosmic role, and furthermore that this love always struggles with an active, embodied hate, and what is really salvation often looks very much like its opposite. Curiously, since neither novelist knew of the other and they are separated by almost seven hundred years, this could be said to be the plot of *The Red Chamber*. Except *The Red Chamber* is a Taoist work. Salvation lies in the quiet power of the stone in the arch, in the action of letting all things find their own level, like water wandering among mountains. Today people would say, "It is impossible to make value judgments of philosophical systems, let alone religious attitudes; they are aesthetic constructs and so, value neuter." This is a lot of hooey. *The Dream of the Red Chamber* is the better novel because it is the truer, the more profoundly humane. *Genji* is true and profound and humane and beautiful, too, but we are not all able to identify ourselves with the insouciant demigod who dips souls from Hell through ten million reincarnations, just, as it were, for fun. On the other hand, there is no question but what we too are part of that astronomical mass of living human beings made of real flesh, sweeping past forever like stardust, and that if we are wise, we will take it easy, like the resting stone and the falling stream.

As a footnote: this Pantheon edition of the *Red Chamber* is not a reprint of either of the two previous translations of the *Hung Lou Meng*, both of which were decided abridgements. It is over twice as long as one, and four times the length of the other, and can be said to be, although somewhat abridged, about as adequate a presentation of the monumental structure of *The Dream of the Red Chamber* as the Western reader is likely to accept. A good deal of care has been taken by the translators to avoid unnecessary exoticism—a comparison of the rendering of proper names in the three versions shows this instantly, and in every way more of the slow, massive lyricism of the original comes through as it never has before. Pearl Buck's rendering of *All Men Are Brothers* is, of course, her finest work and a classic of American prose.

# THE HEROIC OBJECT
# AND FERNAND LÉGER

Suppose the faithful Marmon or Velie, that's been in the family for generations, breaks down in the hills above Figeac, and you coast into town and a helpful *routier* gives you a push into the one garage. Does the mechanic tell you to get rid of that piece of junk? Does he look in vain through his strictly up-to-date Motor Manual? Does he tell you he can't fix it? He does not. He whistles through his teeth, rolls a cigarette, then asks you wistfully for an American cigarette, lights it with profuse thanks, opens the hood, detaches the dodecahedron polymerizer from the reciprocating cam, smiles brightly, says, "Ah, m'sieu, c'est la bonne chance, ce fait rien," and proceeds to make another one, better than the first, using no manuals of any kind and only a pliers and a file.

There are not fifty million mechanics like him, but there are a considerable number, and if it weren't for them France would not be in existence today, and would certainly not have survived the years since 1870. Léger is one of them. He is the man who knows what to do when it breaks, the man who can always make it go.

After the first painting of his apprentice days, he is always completely competent to the task at hand. He knows what he wants to do, and he does it with a machinist's efficiency. It is possible that the tasks he has set himself are not the most complex in the history of painting, but each one is conceived with complete clarity and economy and finished with neatness and dispatch. In fact, it might well be said that Léger's directness has bypassed all those problems of modern painting which are not immediately demonstrable as admitting a simple, rational solution, a manipulative rather than a mentalistic, verbal, expressive solution. It should not be forgotten, in these days when Husserl, Heidegger, and Scheler rule the café *terasses*, that this used to be called the specific French genius. And, for that matter, even the *bagarre* of Saint-Germain is only a formalistic and Tedescan elaboration of attitudes always held in Puteaux or Saint-Denis.

The matter-of-fact competence in the face of life's problems which the French common man has always had, must have or go under, did not need a name from the International Set. Everybody in France who doesn't own five pairs of shoes has always been an existentialist. And so, if they want him, Léger is an existentialist painter. An existentialist of the means at hand. An existentialist without a capital E. Such were the men of the seventeenth century, who made the French spirit out of mathematical models and devices for tracing complex curves, over which the countesses and courtesans swooned in the salons. Such was Racine, expert campanologist of the heart strings, supremely efficient tear-jerker. Such was Rimbaud, the child who applied to decadence the efficiency of a future gun-runner.

We often forget that of the major Cubists, only Braque

and Léger are French. Between them they divide the Gallic utterance of Cubism, soft and hard, feminine and masculine, ingenious and manipulative, the *midinette* and the *mechanicien,* the chef and the peasant. The rest of Cubism is international megalopolitan, except for Picasso's Black Spain of blood and sand.

This is not idle impressionist, exhortative criticism. The qualities which I have mentioned literally overwhelm you in Léger's comprehensive—better, definitive—show [the Museum of Modern Art, New York, 1953]. In room after room the vast paintings take possession of you. You feel like a character in science fiction, a spectator at a congress of intelligent outsized instruments of precision. There is nothing abstract about these pictures. They are portraits of things, of a man, and of a people.

A lot of nonsense, very plastic, has been written and said about Léger, not least of all by himself. Nothing illustrates the fortuitous character of most critical "modern" seeing than the way in which he has been invested, and has been able to garb himself, with the whole panoply of the contemporary formal revolution, or revolutions. Léger is one of the few artists left who still talk about *passéistes,* Renaissance servility to Nature, "photographic realism," the Greeks who could only copy anatomy. Actually, he is not a modern painter at all in the formal sense, but a man of the Renaissance, a composer of objects in representational space, and a Greek of the Greeks, or at least a Roman of the Romans, a painter of isolated human archetypes.

It shows in his first paintings: a portrait of his uncle,

modeled up from a shallow indeterminate background with broken color, Pissarro applied to Carrière; a hillside in Corsica, ochre houses and *terre verte* trees piled up on a hillside like fruit heaped on a platter and seen from above, a problem and a solution which were to satisfy Waroquier for a lifetime. In both pictures the technique is that of an apprentice, but for all that, Léger is perfectly sure of himself even in his mistakes, and the surfaces are certainly modeled. When the uncle was new and the colors bright, he must have more than popped out of the picture.

The next pictures are in what is usually called the African period of Cubism, and it is at this point only that Léger actually joins Picasso and Braque. *Nudes in the Forest* is a minutely painted large canvas completely filled with cubes, tubes, cylinders, and cones of gunmetal blue. It takes Cézanne's injunction literally. The forms of nature are reduced to their geometrical elements. But the elements are represented literally. There is no ambiguity, no interplay of forms. Compare it with Picabia's *Sacre du Printemps*— probably the best picture any of them produced in this period (the Picassos and Braques are very disagreeable productions)—and you will see immediately what I mean. In the Picabia, a blaze of scarlet planes does define the dancers, but no plane stays in place, all weave back and forth, facets first of one form shaped by the attention, then of another. The Léger begins in Mantegna and ends in Wyndham Lewis, and never touches the world of Cubism at all.

Similarly in the heroic age of Cubism, the analytical

period, only the appearance of the paintings of the other Cubists is echoed. The picture surface is completely fragmented into a flicker of values. But the flicker is not the result of the transparencies, interpenetrations, and plastic punning of the *Guitar Players* and portraits of Bass's Ale and *Le Journal;* there is no attempt to create a saturation of space; it is simply filled up with a lot of little sharply rounded objects. Incidentally, the catalog says that the portrait of his uncle is the only representation of an actual person known in Léger's *œuvre.* If the people in *Three Figures* are not portraits, what are they? One is certainly Carco, the woman might be a caricature of Colette of those days, the other face is a masterpiece of portraiture. The grin, sardonic and jolly, even a little tipsy, is the sort of thing you find in self-portraits, but I think Léger had a mustache then.

All the paintings of the analytical period have the same character. The space is filled up, rather than saturated. The planes all stay in one place, the forms are sharply modeled, the "Cubism" itself is merely a geometrical schematization. This is a kind of popular Cubism, a mechanic's idea of what the problem was. As such, it was far more successful than Picasso, Braque, Metzinger, or Gleizes with the public, at least the public of artists around the world. It spread to Italy to the Cubo-Futurists, to Russia, to Chicago to Rudolf Weisenborn, to England to Wyndham Lewis and Wadsworth and their friends. At its worst it died over the mirrors of a thousand Bar Modernes in the postwar (I) world.

Léger's highly articulate remarks about his intentions in these days are very misleading. Of *Woman in Blue* he says, "I obtained rectangles of pure blue and pure red in painting the *Woman in Blue*." So? Raphael obtained triangles of the same colors in the *Madonna of the Meadow*. Both painters modeled their forms in the same way, and, Léger to the contrary, *"Passéiste"* and Modernist, for the same ends, aesthetically speaking.

It is interesting to note that in the more ambitious analytical paintings Léger does seem to be bothered by the bas-relief, piled-up character of his space, and he does try to open it up and cut into it. But to do this he must paint representations of recessions—carved-out slices and corridors, and the step-like figure which from now on he will use again and again. He carries them over into a field in which no one else used them, the postwar period of plane Cubism, of Picasso's *Red Table Cloth*, Braque's *Still Life with Head*, and the finest work of Gris and Marcoussis, a period dominated by the theories of Gleizes.

The great Léger of these days is *The City*. It is, without doubt, a monumental picture, a landmark if not a milestone, in twentieth-century painting, and it is represented in the show by eight or ten different treatments, including the definitive and semi-definitive oils, and a number of closely related watercolor still lifes. Here at last we can see that Léger is not the Douanier of Cubism, he is not a naïf, a primitive. He knows precisely what he is doing. The earliest watercolors, and the painting, *Composition, 1917–1918*, 97x71½, are perfectly straightforward arrangements of planes in bas-relief, piled up toward the spectator—that is, the center plane is the nearest. There is some illusionist modeling, mostly in the oil, only a cylinder in the watercolors. There is a great deal of spiraling movement of form transversely, in the plane of the picture, and even some advance and retreat of planes, all achieved primarily by centrifugal patterning and color snap, by what were called non-illusionist means. They might have been painted by Gleizes in a lively moment.

But when it comes to the painting itself, the final form, all have been subtly altered. The colors are tied to the forms—local colors—the nearest plane is defined by a sharply modeled mauve column which cuts the picture in extreme and mean ratio; behind it two yellow planes recede in conventional perspective, planes of buildings, all brightly colored "for their own sake," recede like stage sets. In the background is a ship; railed staircases lead back in a narrow corridor through the center of the picture, and down them, to complete the illusion, come two black, sharply modeled figures, relatives of the lay figures of Chirico. This may be Cubism but it is not the Cubism of Léger's colleagues. It is the Cubism of Piero della Francesca, perhaps a little reduced. It is as though Léger had deliberately turned his back on the complexities of Gleizes and Gris as trivial.

Once again we have a rejection of the plastic subtleties of intellectual painters in favor of an approach capable of a wide measure of popularization. Out of the work of this period, especially the still lifes, was to come the Suprematism of Ozenfant, some of the Bauhaus painters, particularly Baumeister, and the whole cult of antiseptic modernity in popular art.

*The City* has already taken a long step in this direction. What city? Possibly a modernized Delft of Vermeer, certainly never the Faubourg St. Antoine, the Marais, or La Villette. This is the imaginary city of the movies and the urbanists.

For this reason alone I would prefer, of this period, Léger's *The Great Tug,* a vaguely nautical Gleizes-like mass of colored planes which chooches and chugs through a schematized river landscape. Of course it is a complete contradiction. The "Neo-Cubism" of Léger's colleagues set out to analyze exhaustively the picture area in terms of large planes of color, the surfaces of saturated color volumes, optically retreating and advancing in space. Now this is what Léger says he was doing too. But he was doing nothing of the sort. The tug, the central mass of colored planes, is an object, an abstract object, like a Calder, but representationally though simply painted, and it does not depend on the proportions of the frame directly. On the contrary, it floats in a space which differs little from the background of Piero's *Queen of Sheba.*

Now come the mid-Twenties and Léger's own revolution, "the reinstatement of the object." In other words, he decided to admit what he had been doing all along, and stopped trying to make his paintings look even superficially like other people's. For my taste, these are the best Légers until very recent years. They are completely indi-

231

vidual. They look like nobody else, though lots of other painters try to look like them. And they achieve what Léger can do best, and achieve it superlatively—a wonderful objective immediacy of realization, a true *neue-sächlichkeit* —"Neo-realism" maybe, but the French already had a word for it—*clarté*. Boucher had a clear image like this of *La Petite Morphi*, as Chardin had of pots and pans, and Diderot of Louis XV, and Saint-Just of Louis XVI. This is the virtue that has kept France great, as once it made her strong.

This is the period of the heroic human figures, beginning with the *Mechanic* and the *Three Women*, including *Woman with Book* and *The Readers*. They have been called impersonal abstractions. But they are abstractions only in the sense that Hans and Fritz and Mama and the Captain are abstractions. They are perfect idealizations of universal French types. They have been compared to Poussin, but they are certainly very shallow Poussin. To me they look more like Roman funerary bas-relief, and they have the same archetypical character as the best Roman portraiture. After them come the medallion-like pictures of the late Twenties, most of them rather wittily, and certainly very originally, bifurcated. I like best *The Mirror*, and it is certainly typical, in its wit, its polish, its enormous self-confidence. Now the craftsman knows his craft by heart. It is his heart. His highest spiritual experience is the sense of absolute competence in the face of the problems of the conquest of matter. Cubism, and the problems of modern space

232

architecture, are ignored completely. These are not even bas-reliefs, they are cameos.

So, the next period—of "free color," by which Léger does not mean dissociated color moving as color volume, but just free color, applied as it struck his fancy; and "free form," that is, painting built without a base, floating in air. In part, this latter development is a protest against Picasso, whose compositions all depend on their enormous specific gravity. But Léger's forms do not really float in the "free space" of the space cadets and the Baroque ceilings. They revolve around a center, without top or bottom, like medals—still the same approach. Although the besetting bas-relief is attacked by reducing much of the form to purely linear relationships, they are never the linear swoops and plunges of either Sesshu or Tiepolo. They are always exactly there where the painter put them. I think, curiously enough, the most successful is not the famous *The Divers*, but the quite simple *Chinese Juggler*.

During this period, too, Léger was developing his alphabet of human types. It was then he began—to work on it for nineteen years—his *Three Musicians*, three *numeros* from a *bal musette*, the Fourteenth of July on the Boulevard La Chapelle. It is an independently conceived and painted picture, but no one could miss the implied criticism of Picasso's internationalized, *déracinés*, Ballet Russe ogres.

And this brings us to the culmination, paintings of pure human archetypes, very human, very pure, and very localized to a class and a land, as is Léger himself. In a way the accomplishment of Léger's later life is not unlike that of

233

William Butler Yeats, who was able to achieve in his old age a whole heroic mythos, the kind of an endowment only a Heroic Age gives most peoples, for the ungrateful Irish. *Leisure, The Great Julie, The Chinese Juggler,* and the rest are close to being Platonic Ideas of the French common people. If you doubt it, ponder *Adam and Eve,* represented as hero and heroine of the *théâtre de foire,* snake charmers, street performers such as you might see any sultry August, in a neighborhood *place* anywhere in France, the immortal parents of Little Remi, Vitalis, and their dogs and the monkey, Joli-Coeur.

And finally, there is the great picture, *The Builders,* on whose title and subject many philosophical and sociological speculations and reveries might be based. These are the builders of France, after another time, out of so many years of war, disorder, and betrayal. And plastically Léger has moved on a little. The space is deep and open, with interchanging diagonals. One is reminded of Signorelli, but a Signorelli in which all the figures are standing at attention. It may be Egypt applied to the High Renaissance. But neither Egypt nor the High Renaissance produced a great many more profoundly moving pictures of human beings.

# THE PLAYS
# OF YEATS

The collected plays of William Butler Yeats have recently [1953] been issued by Macmillan in a complete edition that sells for $5.50.* The former edition, to which this adds five later plays, was published in 1935 and soon went out of print.

Yeats is certainly the greatest poet of our time. I think I can say this without any qualification. There is no French poet who can compare with him, and there's no poet in any other language who comes anywhere near him.

Yeats began writing late romantic, *art nouveau* verse. He made a great deal of his association with the Rhymers' Club, with Dowson and Lionel Johnson. Actually, he didn't write very much like them. He wrote more like Maeterlinck, who is the *art nouveau* writer par excellence and who was a part of that whole movement of artistic nationalism typified by the Provençal poet, Mistral.

Yeats's whole mind was saturated with vapors and languors, an indefinite, sentimentally mystical coloring which is seen in Maeterlinck at its most extreme and which survived in a trivial popular form in Lord Dunsany, whose plays sound like parodies of the early Yeats. This was true

---

* This is a direct transcript of a weekly book program on KPFA, San Francisco's non-commercial listener-supported radio station. It was delivered without notes or preparation and has not been "edited."

of Yeats's poetry. It was even truer of his plays.

In the arts the only painters who survive from that period to represent the same tendencies are Puvis de Chavannes and Maurice Denis, and even, in a peculiar rough-hewn way, Gauguin. In music, Debussy, Ravel, Delius are part of the world. And this is an unsatisfactory world. Yeats never fitted these garments very well. He always seemed to be bursting out of them, and he very early started to make an artistic credo and a philosophy for himself. His philosophy is found in his book, *A Vision*, a book essential to the understanding of Yeats. His poetry and his plays are filled with symbols and exemplifications of his philosophical and mystical beliefs.

The early plays in this Celtic twilight idiom, like *The Countess Cathleen*, *The Shadowy Waters*, *The King's Threshold*, *Pot of Broth*, *The Land of Heart's Desire*, *Cathleen ni Houlihan*, I played in my salad days in the little theater. And the thing that they were that Maeterlinck was not is theatrical. They come across the footlights with surprising impact and they are beautifully manageable within their own décor. The burlap sets and blue canvas smocks and gold-painted leather Celtic jerkins of the early Yeats, seen behind a scrim under pale lights, green on one side and lavender on the other, are really very effective. It's not anywhere near as silly as it sounds. These are very moving plays theatrically—very difficult to ruin.

Yeats' plays are seldom given any more. In the old days they were given by very bad little theater groups, yet they stood up and walked across the footlights and grappled with the audience in a way that only the work of the greatest playwrights does. Their first appearance of slightness and sentimentality is misleading. Once you accept the idiom, some of the lines are very beautiful. *The Shadowy Waters,* for instance, which is in a long romantic line, has a dusky, twilight, and jeweled bronze quality. It's really a misty echo of the Irish Bronze Age that comes across.

Then Yeats became familiar with Japanese drama through the translations of Ernest Fenollosa, and Pound went to work at Yeats' home putting Fenollosa's translations of the Noh Plays into shape. These plays had a determinative influence on Yeats. As was also the case with the English poet, Sturge Moore, he was simply overwhelmed by the simplicity and by the new dramatic insights afforded by Noh. Now, Noh drama does not rise to a climax like *Hamlet* or *East Lynne.* It creates an atmosphere, but it creates an atmosphere in very sharp, definite terms—imagistic terms as they called them in those days—not in the shadowy way that *The Shadowy Waters* does, for instance. Noh creates a dramatic atmosphere of unresolved tension, or unresolved longings, or irresolution in the dramatic sense—and then this dramatic situation is resolved by a kind of aesthetic realization which evolves from the dramatic situation as its own archetype. This resolution takes the form of a dance, which can best be compared to a crystal of sugar dropping into a supersaturated solution. All the sugar that is held in solution will crystallize around the introduced crystal and form rock sugar until the solution is

237

no longer saturated.

What eventuates is not a sense of resolved climax, but a sense of realized significance. This is a different thing— not the Aristotelian pattern of tragic drama as we have known it in the West. Yeats was simply enraptured by this discovery and used it from then on. Sturge Moore wrote a number of Noh plays at the same time. His was a more pedestrian mind—a very high-toned pedestrian mind. In many ways he was an extremely skilled poet. You could certainly call Moore's plays mellifluous, but it's interesting to compare them with Yeats. There is a universal reduction of scale. You are in a smaller and lesser world. Yeats' dance-dramas, on the other hand, compare very favorably with the greatest Japanese Noh. There is a genuine realization of heroic archetype. You feel the same way at the parting of Lancelot and Guinevere or at the episodes of the *Iliad* or the episodes of Lady Murasaki's *Genji* and the Chinese *Dream of the Red Chamber,* the episodes of *Don Quixote* or the *Ramayana* and *Mahabharata.* You are dealing with human experience reduced to pure archetypes, the sort of thing that people called deities and demigods and heroes. Yeats really does achieve this purity and nobility.

This is what makes major writing major—the ability to project human experience against a heroic background, to pour human thought and motivation and life into figures which exemplify the universal tragic situation of all men everywhere. Myths. Comparative mythology is comparable —Greek, Welsh, Polynesian, Irish, Japanese—because all men are, beyond all moral relativism, comparable. All

238

works of great art have this in common—the ability to realize human experience in its most archetypical and ideal
forms.

Yeats' language changed at this time too. The change
took place in his plays before it did in his poems. He came
to realize that the greatest poetic speech was an enormously
purified common speech—that the lingo of *art nouveau,*
the twilight imagery and pseudo-medieval diction ultimately derived from William Morris and his followers,
could not achieve heroic ends. Nothing sounds less like the
parting of Lancelot and Guinevere in the *Morte d'Arthur*
than the language of William Morris very carefully modeled on the *Morte d'Arthur.* John Middleton Synge, another
of the major leaders of the Irish revival, studied carefully
the speech of the peasants of the Aran Islands and the west
of Ireland generally, and by using this speech pretty much
as they did, by using the vocabulary, the idiom's syntax,
and even saying the things they did, he was able to sound
very much like Malory or even Homer, and (he translated
Villon) like Villon.

Under the influence of Synge and Lady Gregory, who
was also interested in the use of folk speech to recover for
poetry its original exaltation, Yeats developed a whole new
language for himself. He went far beyond them in doing
this. Yeats is an incomparably greater writer than Lady
Gregory, although there is certainly nothing wrong with
Lady Gregory. She is good at her own level and a considerably greater writer in some ways than Synge, because she
is so much less sentimental.

239

The thing that vitiates a good deal of Synge is a kind of leprechaun sentimentality. In spite of his excellent theories and his careful use of pure language and reduction of plot to situations of great dramatic simplicity, Synge is, nevertheless, a little too sentimental. Incidentally, Tennessee Williams has made a reputation for himself in recent years by doing nothing more than reworking the plots of *The Playboy of the Western World*, *The Tinker's Wedding*, and so forth. Synge used a basic plot situation which is to my mind a little dishonest, because it deals with modern revolt. That is, it's a sort of Ibsen in the far west of Ireland, and as we all know today, the problems of Nora and Hedda were limited in time and place.

The best plays, the greatest achievement of Yeats, are the dance-dramas dealing with the life of the Irish Heroic Age hero, Cuchulain. Best of these, perhaps, are *At the Hawk's Well*, and, one of the last things Yeats wrote, *The Death of Cuchulain*. It is difficult to say—*The Only Jealousy of Emer* is probably their equal. All achieve a purity and intensity quite unlike anything in the modern theater. We should remember that in the days in which they were being written, the advanced theater meant to most people the vulgar racket of German expressionism. There are no errors, lapses, or gaucheries in these plays of Yeats. Formally, they are so extremely purified that any fault, if it existed, would protrude like a mustache, not on the face of the Mona Lisa, but on the face of Mademoiselle Pogany. As far as the West is concerned, Yeats had, like a spider, to draw his material out of himself, and yet he worked with the instinctive assurance of a man with a thousand years of tradition behind him. It all looks so easy, like the sword-play of the Japanese swordsmen taught by the effortless discipline of Zen. Yeats perfects and sharpens his dramatic instrument and drives it home with absolute impact, like the swordsman whose weapon finds curves and crevices in space along which it slips, guiding the hand of the wielder, and beheading the opponent, who goes on duelling for some seconds until a sudden rough movement on his part tumbles his head from his body.

Besides this, the choruses of these plays are amongst the very greatest poems that Yeats ever wrote. Although they are integral to the plays, they also stand perfectly by themselves. I believe they are superior to the more fashionable poems of Yeats's later work. They have the unbothered simplicity of folk speech in its highest utterance—as one might imagine, not one of the characters in Synge's plays, but a real girl of the Aran Islands speaking of her lover dead at sea. They achieve all the things Yeats sought for in poetry and they avoid his characteristic distractions. They really have mythic power, simplicity, directness, mana, Otto's "sense of the holy." In the age of Seami or Aeschylus, this would make Yeats a very considerable figure. In an age given over to people like Christopher Fry, Maxwell Anderson, T. S. Eliot, Tennessee Williams, and Eugene O'Neill, he is absolutely unique. To say that he is the greatest English dramatist of our time is simply to say that he is the best of a bad lot. He is a good dramatist for any language and for any time.

241

# INDEX